The beginner's guide to the microscope, with a section on mounting slides

Charles E Heath

THE BEGINNER'S GUIDE TO THE MICROSCOPE

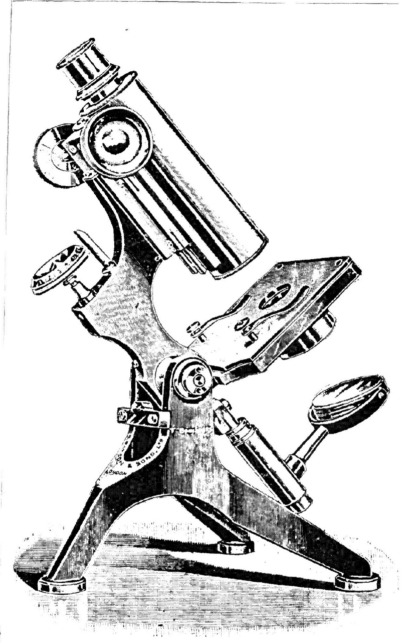

An Ideal Microscope to Standard Sizes.
Capable of future additions, if required.

THE BEGINNER'S GUIDE

TO

THE MICROSCOPE

WITH A SECTION ON MOUNTING SLIDES

BY

CHAS. E. HEATH, F.R.M.S.

FULLY ILLUSTRATED

LONDON :

PERCIVAL MARSHALL & CO.,

66, FARRINGDON STREET, LONDON, E.C.4.

CONTENTS.

———

THE BEGINNER'S GUIDE TO THE MICROSCOPE.

CHAPTER I.

INTRODUCTION.

MICROSCOPY is usually regarded as a science in itself, and one of unusual difficulty. Although its perfect mastery involves a thorough knowledge of optics and considerable acquaintance with mathematical formulæ it is not so much a science in itself as a servant of all the sciences There is hardly a science, profession, or trade to which it cannot in some way contribute by enlarging our senses to perceive the unseen, or by assisting our powers of observation to resolve the seen with an understanding of its uses. It is not what is seen, but what is observed, that is of value; and a very elementary use of the instrument undoubtedly increases the power of observation, thus serving a use by cultivating the powers of the observer in his other walks of life.

We are not here concerned with microscopy as a science, nor in a positive sense as even an aid to science, but to enable an ordinary man in an ordinary way to interest himself and his friends by giving sufficient instruction to make him capable of seeing and shewing some of the hidden wonders that are around us.

There are far more intense dramas played in one's own home than at first sight appear, and when the habits and ends of the tiny players are understood their contemplation becomes more interesting than the dramas we pay to see. Even with the naked eye, after the habit of observation is cultivated, one can see acting where death is the penalty of the incompetent hunted, or starvation the penalty of the incompetent hunter. The plot is the same: Eat, or be eaten; establish, or fail to establish, the next generation; but the varieties presented of this plot are endless.

Fig. 2.—Light Microscope with Tripod Foot.

The principal difficulty felt by a beginner in attempting to use a microscope is that its uses are so varied and its scope so universal, that the adjustments appear so complicated, the reason for them not being understood, that he does not know where and how to begin.

There are several good books which are most useful when the initial difficulties are surmounted, and this handbook is not intended to compete with these more ambitious and expensive works. It is simply designed to smooth the road for the absolute novice; enabling him to enter afterwards if he so desire into more strictly scientific work, and to study the more advanced books with ease, and enlarging his capacity to acquire future knowledge.

If, however, he proceeds no farther than this book will take him, it will secure intelligent amusement and

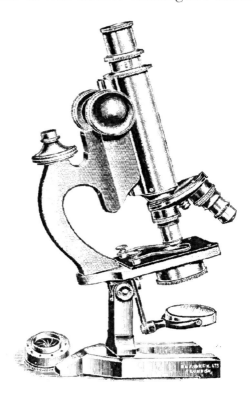

Fig. 3.—Student's Microscope with Horseshoe Foot.

rational recreation by the use of a simple instrument on objects close at hand. It will open his eyes even without previous optical knowledge or experience to the wonders of the world with which he is in contact everywhere, and will assist him to realise that nature is as great, looking as it were inwards, as it is in the enormous magnitudes seen in looking upwards or out-

wards. The celestial phenomena with which we are
at least superficially acquainted are no greater in kind

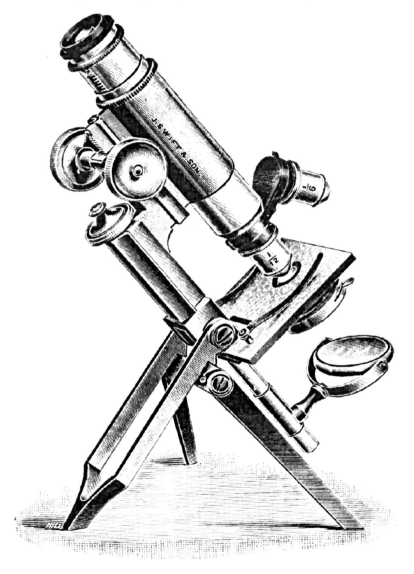

Fig. 4.—A Good Folding Microscope.

than the marvellous complexities of the indefinitely
little.

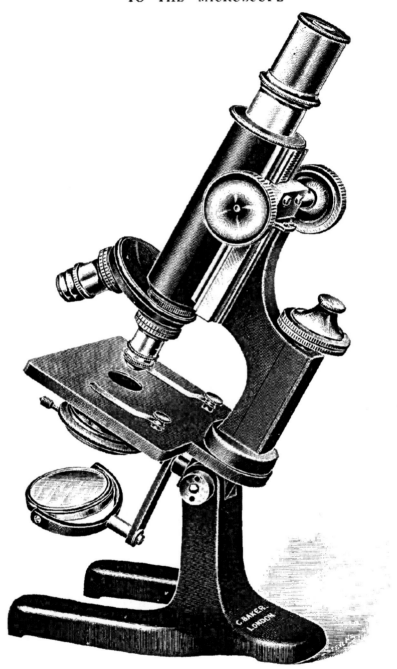

Fig. 5.—Typical Microscope.· Horseshoe Foot with Sleeve
Fitting Understage.

All realise that both exist, but the greater in magnitude is observed whilst the smaller is overlooked owing to its extreme minuteness. This defect of our powers is remedied by the microscope owing to the assistance

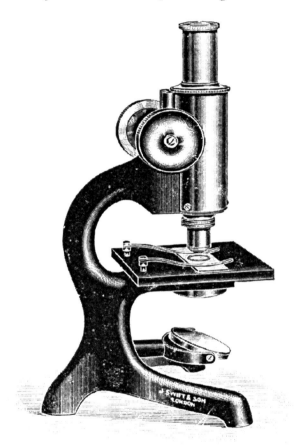

Fig. 6.—A Cheap Microscope of Modern Form.
Non-inclinable Stand.

given by the instrument to the human eye.

It is unfortunate that the tyro almost invariably rushes to use the highest powers he can obtain, and this, unless kept in check, leads to disappointment and disgust. We should begin with generals and descend to particulars. Start with the lowest powers, which are easy to use, and easy to manipulate on the instrument, and when a general idea of various objects is attained one can look for detail with greater magnification.

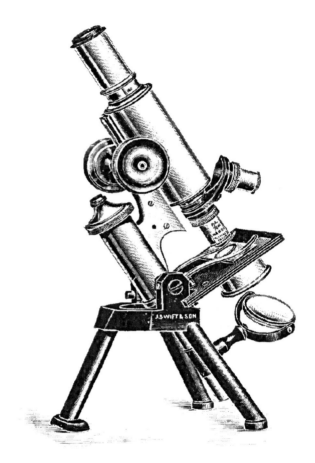

Fig. 7.- Student's Microscope with Tripod Foot.

The apprenticeship in using the low powers for the first few months is a training for the use of the higher ones, but it must be noted that empty magnification alone of an object is not desirable and that the lowest power which will reveal what we wish to see is the

right power to use. The higher the power the smaller
the portion which can be seen at one time, and our

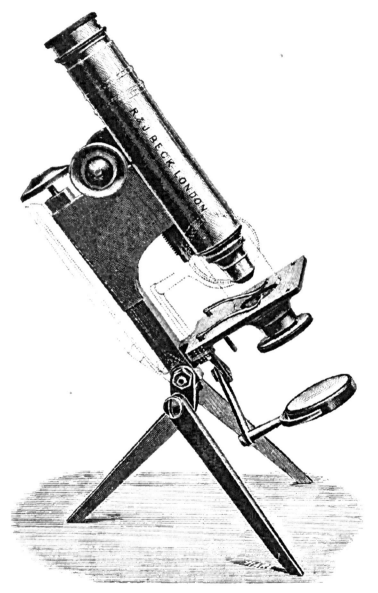

Fig. 8. - Very Light Folding Microscope.

general idea of the form under observation suffers.

The highest powered lenses money can buy do not reveal the ultimate constitution of matter, but much that is instructive of its organisation into forms is shewn by the medium and low powers in use.

If the would-be microscopist lives in London. he should apply for a ticket to any good firm of opticians, which will admit him to the Quekett Microscopical Club on one of their " Gossip " nights, which are the fourth Tuesday in each month. He will see there exactly how a microscope should be used and how objects are shown at their best. It is a Club in the true sense, as information is freely given, and the writer is greatly indebted to its members for his own knowledge of the subject. A visitor will find specialists in every kind of microscopic manipulation, and his difficulties would soon vanish under the kindly tuition so kindly, if informally, given.

CHAPTER II.

THE MICROSCOPE DESCRIBED.

The microscope described.—The term microscope is sometimes applied to a simple hand lens or magnifying glass, which is most useful in its place for a preliminary examination of an object, and should be possessed by every microscopist, but in this book the term microscope will be used to signify the compound microscope in which, instead of looking directly through a lens at the object, one looks at its magnified image produced by one lens and examined by another.

The history of the microscope and its development has no place here, as it has been fully treated elsewhere; but we have to do with the modern instrument as usually made, which is really one in form, although various modifications in design and arrangement are manufactured.

Fig. 9.—Hand Magnifying Glass, or Pocket Lens.

A compound microscope consists essentially of two systems of lenses so arranged in exact alignment that the image formed behind the front system of lenses—called the objective—is thrown into a position whence it can be viewed by a second system of lenses called the eyepiece or ocular. This ocular further magnifies the original enlarged image, and the combined magnification of the two lenses is transferred to the eye, which assumes from its nature and construction that the image exists as an object at the normal distance of clear vision, usually ten inches, when the eye *appears* to perceive it.

For the purpose of comfort in use and adjustment of focus, which has to be very exact and rigid when found, the arrangement known generally as a stand is required, and although there is much variety in outward appearance, there is a great similarity in real form, as whatever the means taken to provide the motions, the adjustments required are the same in all

There must be some means of varying the distance of tubes from the stage, and for this is provided two kinds of movements in the same vertical direction, a rapid one usually working by rack and pinion, but sometimes by a sliding tube, and a very fine slow movement which is variously attained, sometimes by a fine screw alone, sometimes by a fine screw working through a lever, and sometimes by one screw working within another so that the resulting motion is the difference between the two screws. There are also cams and rollers, but all that is necessary to observe in use is that the turning of one milled head in some way gives a delicate and smooth movement through a very small vertical distance.

The tubes carrying the lenses usually slide inside each other in order that the distance between the lenses may be varied This is because some objectives are constructed to give the more perfect image with a ten-inch tube and others with a six-and-a-half-inch tube By having the draw tube it is possible to use either kind Incidentally, drawing out and lengthening the tube gives greater magnification, and in low

powers it can be so used to get intermediate enlarge-
ments, but for objective lenses above one inch in power
this method should not be used, as the less perfect
image due to wrong tube length becomes apparent.

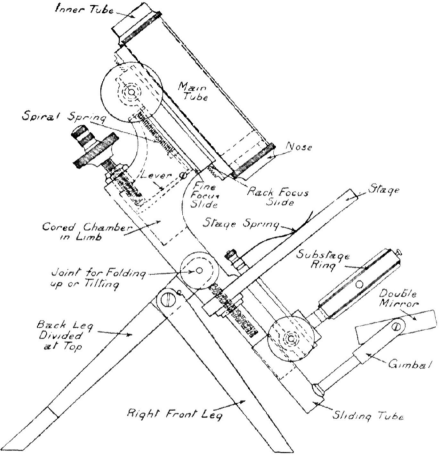

Fig. 10.—Microscope with Names of its Parts.

The lower end of tube is screwed with a thread to
take the objectives, all of which, by makers of repute,
are interchangeable on to any other make of instrument. The upper end has several standards, the eyepiece simply dropping easily into the top end of draw
tube.

The size most in use is the No. 1 R.M.S Standard, and is the cheapest to buy, and in almost universal use except on the very largest stands.

The limb is that portion of the framework which carries the slides and tubes above the stage, and from which the adjustments just described are worked

The stage is the horizontal platform on which the objects are carried, and is fitted either with detachable clips or, in expensive instruments, with mechanical methods of shifting the object, and for special purposes may carry a revolving plate as well; but these luxuries are not usual, nor even desirable for a beginner.

At the back of the stage is a hinged joint by which the upper portion of the instrument may be inclined, sometimes merely friction-tight and at others having a clamping screw.

The base is varied in form, but all the shapes can be resolved into one of three types: The folding leg is best if the instrument is to be carried about, but is not usually as rigid when set up as the others; the solid tripod foot, which is the best and firmest under all circumstances; and the horseshoe foot, which has the advantage of a smaller case if taken out, and slightly more room to manipulate any apparatus under the stage if such is used; but it is not so stable laterally, and unless very heavy is easily knocked over when set up.

The mirror is carried on a tailrod or arm projecting downwards below the stage. Its function is to reflect the light from window or lamp upwards through the stage opening on to the object. It can be canted or swivelled in any direction, and should be tight enough to remain where placed, and not be shifted in position by slight vibration. It is usually double, having a concave surface on one side and a plain surface on the other The concave should be used for low-powered lenses without a condenser beneath the stage, but when a condensing lens is fitted the plain side should be used unless in exceptional circumstances, as converging light as reflected from a concave mirror has the same effect as interposing another lens into the condenser, thus shortening its focus and perhaps rendering it useless for the purpose in view.

The understage is a sleeved fitting to carry simple forms of condensing lenses, spot lens, and polarizer. It takes the form of a short tube fixed to the under side of stage, and the proper diameter is 1.527, just over one-and-a-half inches inside. It is inferior to a proper substage, but less expensive, whilst capable of showing much that the beginner requires. It has only a small range of vertical adjustment, and except in rare cases no centering arrangement.

The substage is a bracket fitted beneath the stage in such a way that the condensing lenses, etc., are held in a centering ring which by a rack and pinion

Fig. 11.—Abbe Condenser for Understage.

movement can be raised or lowered as desired. This form of substage is most necessary for high-class work, but the preceding arrangement of a sleeved fitting will suffice for all but the most advanced manipulation.

The condenser.—This is a system of lenses for condensing light from the mirror and focussing exactly on the object.

In the form shewn it is called the Abbé condenser, which, with proper use and arrangement in a suitable substage, can take the place of all the contrivances which at one time were necessary to illuminate the object, as it can be used in various ways to get the effect desired.

Fig. 12 gives the optical part only. Fig. 13 gives it with the mechanical part to carry patch stops and

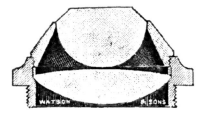

Fig. 12.—Optical Part of Abbe Illuminator. 1·20 N.A.

diaphragms. Fig. 11 shows the form for pushing up from below for the simple sleeved underfitting, and Fig. 13 the form for slipping in from above into a complete centering substage apparatus.

Fig. 13.—Abbe Condenser Mounted for Substage.

A condenser is not required for low power work on transparent objects, but the diaphragm of the mechanical part will be wanted, and to get the beautiful effects of " dark ground illumination " at its best some form of condensing lens is necessary.

The mechanical part also carries a swing-out ring, which takes various coloured glasses as light modifiers as may be at the time desirable.

There are for advanced work other forms of condenser of more expensive and complicated character, but which are not required by the beginner. The Abbe form illustrated here is easiest to use as it does not require such delicate adjustments and precision of centering, and if properly managed it will show all that the tyro can reasonably expect to see.

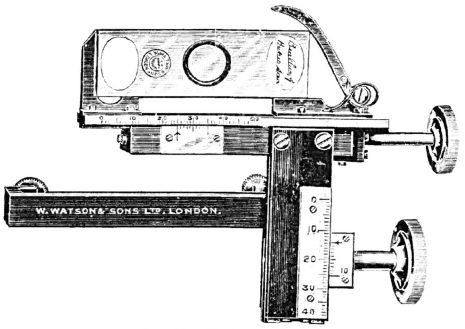

Fig. 14.—Mechanical Stage.

These may be built into the Instrument, or made detachable. They are only required for very precise work. Convenient to use, but by no means essential.

Nosepiece.—The bottom end of main tube of microscope which receives the objective. Separate nosepieces which receive two, three, or more objectives can be supplied which rotate on a central screw, bringing either or any of the lenses into the optic axis as required. If accurately made they are very useful, enabling a low power to be used to find and centre an object, when a higher power for more detailed examination can be brought to bear.

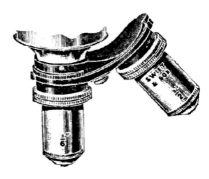

Fig. 15.—Double Nosepiece for changing Objectives.

They seldom, however, bring the centre of one lens into exact coincidence with the centre of another, partly because the lens centres themselves do not always coincide with the screw threads, and partly because the nosepieces cannot be made with sufficient precision.

" *Bull's Eye.*"—A lens convex on one face and plane on the other, with various jointed motions to allow change of position. It is used in various ways explained on a later page.

An Iris diaphragm is an arrangement of leaves which can be opened or closed at any time by sliding a lever projecting through a slot in its side to increase or diminish the size of opening beneath the stage. The desired result of varying the size of opening sometimes takes the form of various sized holes in a rotating disc. Its true use is to regulate the angle of cone of the light passed rather than its quantity. The quantity should be regulated by a screen, as decreasing the angle of cone beyond certain limits reduces the definition of the objective lens as well as reducing the quantity of light. On low powers, however, it scarcely interferes with the performance of a lens unless reduced to an extreme degree, as these are narrow angle lenses and do not

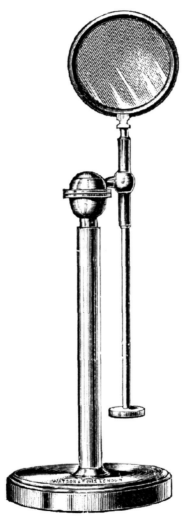

Fig. 16.—Bull's Eye for Condensing Light.

suffer materially by a reduced aperture in substage diaphragm. An adjustable diaphragm is sometimes fitted above the objective lens and is then called a " Davis " shutter. By closing this the available aperture of lens is reduced and increased penetration is obtained, so

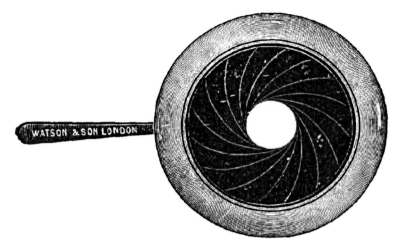

Fig. 17.—Iris Diaphragm.

that objects of appreciable thickness may appear in focus throughout their depth in one view. It does so, however, at the expense of a slight general loss all over as the resolving power of the lens is diminished with decrease of aperture.

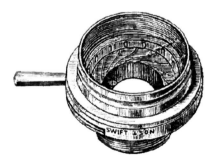

Fig. 18.—" Davis " Shutter, or Diaphragm above Objective Lens.

The lamp.—For work with low power during daylight a lamp is not necessary. At night, however, some form of lamp must be used, and any flat flame lamp will do if some form of shade is devised to keep direct light from the eye.

The usual lamp for microscope use when made for the purpose is like Fig. 19, where the lamp can be raised or lowered, and is fitted with an adjustable shade.

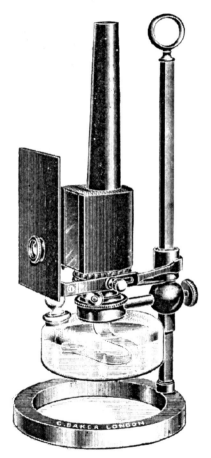

Fig. 19.—The usual style of Oil Lamp for Microscopical use.

A lamp which can be recommended is an incandescent gas lamp fitted up as shewn in Fig. 20, as with a shade of this kind various stock size glasses or light modifiers $3 \times 1\frac{1}{2}$ can be inserted as desired. For dark ground illumination the extra power of the gas light is preferable to an oil lamp, and its white colour is very welcome, as the image can be made very brilliant, even if the object be somewhat dense.

A pendant electric light, if it can be lowered on its flexible cord, will suffice for low power illumination and give every satisfaction. For critical illumination,

Fig. 20.—Incandescent Gas Lamp.

however, which is mentioned later, the ordinary filament lamp is not suitable, as the image of the light focussed by the condenser on the object is a reduced picture in the form of the loops and cannot be made to give an evenly illuminated field of view.

The binocular microscope.—The binocular, or double barrelled microscope was at one time much coveted and used, but latterly the desire for short tubes and portable microscopes appears to have ousted it from popular favour. In one sense this is a great pity, as

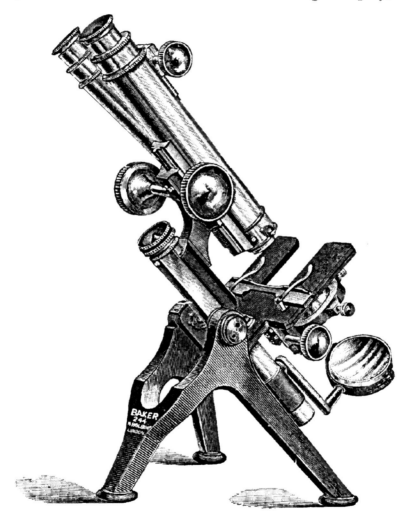

Fig. 21.—Binocular Microscope for Stereoscopic Vision.

if a microscope is to be used at home and on low power work, there is nothing to beat the binocular form if one can afford it. Its sole disadvantage, other than non-portability, is that to split the image in half, as it does, and convey it half to each eye necessitates a ten-inch tube. Now a ten-inch tube with an ordinary table and an ordinary chair makes the eyepiece too high for observation sitting down One wants a lower table, a higher chair, or must stand up.

The binocular microscope gets its two images by a prism which extends over half the distance across the tube behind the objective lens, and conveys one half of the image by reflection into another path than the direct, whilst the direct rays go straight up the tube in the usual way. This gives a solid effect, and as very few of the objects viewed with low powers are thin and flat, but have a definite thickness, one gets a much greater conception of structural form than with the single type of instrument It cannot well be used for powers higher than half inch, but is suitable for all lower ones, and for amateur use on unprepared subjects, or living specimens lighted with the bull's-eye, or side reflector, it is superb As eyes vary in their distance apart the binocular microscope is furnished with sliding tubes at the eyepiece end which diverge outwardly to give greater distance between by raising, or to suit narrower eye separation by lowering them.

A binocular always carries a little stop at the bottom which actuates the position of the prism fitted just above the objective This slides in and out, and when the prism is withdrawn the microscope becomes an ordinary monocular instrument, and if otherwise suitable can be used for the highest powers.

The binocular microscope is very good used with " dark ground illumination " for all kinds of pond life examined alive and in its natural condition. There is not only the charm of having both eyes occupied and equally trained, but the gratification of seeing stereoscopically. Any person acquainted with the difference of seeing through a stereoscope and looking at only one of the photographs separately can easily imagine the enhanced effect of a good binocular microscope.

CHAPTER III.

HOW AN IMAGE IS FORMED

How an image is formed —All real images formed by light are aerial images, and exist just the same, whether the screen on which they are received be present or not. The screen simply makes them visible. Before we can understand how the aerial image in the microscope is formed without a screen on which to receive it we must endeavour to grasp the reason for the image existing at all, and to do this we must learn a little of the elementary subject of light Light is assumed to be caused by a vibration in a substance existing everywhere to which the name ether has been given It is presumed that the vibrations take place along definite straight lines. and it is also presumed that the course of a ray of light would always be straight unless some substance capable of turning it from its course is interposed. Any transparent substance has its own capacity of bending aside a light ray, called its refractive index, but the only substance which we have to consider at this stage is glass Even glass can vary in different specimens owing to its different content, and we shall see presently that this important variation of density is made use of to its uttermost by combining different forms of lenses to produce the perfect image in the microscope.

The way an image is formed by a magic lantern is fairly well understood, and the photographic camera is everywhere, and most persons at some time or other have seen the ground glass screen with its inverted image A magic lantern image is also inverted, but this is not so obvious to the observer as the operator inserts his slides upside down. Let us first see how an image, not very perfect, can be formed without a lens. If a cardboard box, white inside, has a small hole punctured with a coarse needle in the middle of one end, and such end exposed towards an external object in bright sunshine, or even if pointed at a bright light indoors, a feeble image of the object before the pinhole will be formed on the inside back of the box. The box has become a camera. This can be seen easily

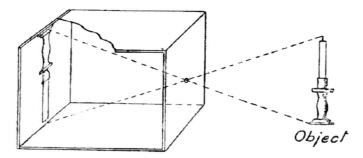

Fig. 22.—An Image formed by a Pinhole.

if a hole screened from direct light be made in the side of the box so that the inside of the back, opposite to the pinhole, is visible. We see that the ray of light emanating from the bottom of the object passes through the pinhole and impinges on the back of the box at the top. Similarly, a ray from the top passes through the hole and reaches the back of the box at the bottom. The same with either side, and with every ray which proceeds from every point of the object reaches a corresponding portion, and their cumulative effect is to build an image on the inside of the back of box. This image is imperfect and vague as each point of the object does not reach a corresponding point in the image, but a disc a trifle larger than the pinhole—and all these discs are more or less superposed on each other—and hence rather confused.

It is also very feeble, as the diameter of pinhole being so small the amount of light passed is small also. Now let us see what happens with the camera, the ground glass screen of which is in the back of the box and can be seen from the outside, so no light reaches the screen from the front except that which assists to build up this image. Now every ray of light proceeding in all directions outwardly from every point of the illuminated object does not reach the lens, but those which do reach the lens are greater in quantity than the light passed by the pinhole, and in the proportion of their relative areas the image is brighter and

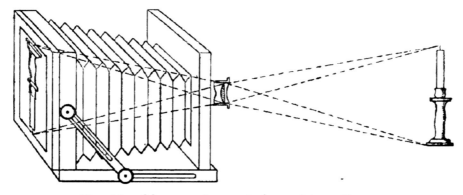

Fig. 23.—How an Image is formed in a Camera.

their relative area of aperture is as the squares of their diameter. But this is not all. The lens does not, as the pinhole does, allow a greater diffusion disc if the screen be near the focus of the lens, and if the exact position of the focus of the lens be found at which these rays reach their smallest point, the diffusion disc becomes so small as to present a sharp image as a whole. The distance at which a lens forms its image is one conjugate focus of the lens, and the smallest diffusion disc is called its anti-point. The same happens with an optical lantern. The slide, upside down, is placed in position from which light can be passed through it, and a lens in front is moved or focussed till the point is found where the rays are condensed into points on the distant screen, which the eye sees as a whole and receives as a picture. There is almost exact similarity between these instances and the image formed by the microscope, although there is no screen

No person who thinks of what takes place in this light of regarding the matter can doubt that the images are still present in the same places in both instances if the screen or ground glass were removed. This image, called an aerial image, is still there although too large to be taken into the pupil of the eye as a whole at one time. It is a real image, and really exists, but without the screen we cannot perceive it as such. But if a system of lenses brought it down as a whole to pass into the pupil of the eye it could be seen as a whole. Now this is what the eye lens does in the microscope. The aerial image is condensed again as though it appeared to come from the directions as to size in which it really exists, and the eye, which always refers rays of light to straight lines refers all points in the image along the lines from which it appears to come The normal distance of distinct vision being about ten inches we appear to see the image as though it were that distance away from the eye.

It will be perceived from this that the greater the bundle of rays received and brought to a point, the brighter will be the image, and this brilliancy is in proportion to the area open in the lens. Hence, lenses of large aperture pass more light than those of small aperture There is, however, another aspect of the work done by the lens It is found that light, when sent through an object containing very fine structure, is bent or spread out in fan-like form from every fine point however small in such structure. This is called " diffraction," and when the light from a condenser

is focussed on a transparent object there is not only
the shadow picture of that object to be found in light
and shade on our aerial screen, but the lens receives
all these diffraction fans of light which can pass its
aperture and brings them into proper focus at their
anti-point   Now, the larger the aperture, the greater
the diameter of the diffracted fan received and the

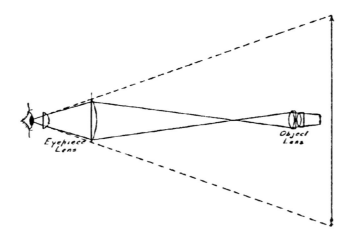

Fig. 24   How an Image is formed in the Microscope.

finer the quality of the built up image. It is found
that the wide aperture lenses are capable of much
superior definition than those of narrow angle lenses,
and for obtaining pictures of an object lying all in one
plane and very thin the former are much more desirable.   This remark refers, of course, to the higher
powers mostly, although in low power work lenses of
large aperture define better than those of small.   The
lenses of small aperture have the advantage if objects
are thick, inasmuch that the cone of light received
being more pointed owing to the narrower base, a
greater thickness of the object, or several planes of the
object can be passably good focus at one time   This
is owing to the smaller diffusion disc, which does not

enlarge so rapidly as the image goes out of focus, the taper of the cone of light being sharper. The narrow angle lens, however, workmanship being equal, does not define in any one plane as well as the wide angle lens does. A reference to Fig. 24 will shew the part the eyepiece and objective lens take in doing their work. A single ray from each end of the object is represented for simplicity, but it must not be overlooked that a bundle of rays equal to aperture of lens proceed from each and every point in the object as a cone of rays and are condensed as another cone of rays to the corresponding point in the resultant image.

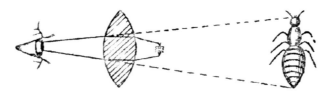

Fig. 25.   How a Hand Lens seems to Magnify.

The rays cross on their way, as light can pass through light without mutual disturbance of any of it; they reach the eyepiece where the inner or field lens bends them in again and the image is formed in the air between the lenses of the eyepiece. They pass on through the outer or eye lens, where their direction is again changed so that the whole bundle can enter the pupil of the eye, and they enter in such a direction that the eye sees it as an image, as a whole; the referring it to a larger one of ten inches distance being a function of the eye or the brain, which translates visual impressions into mental conceptions. In a microscope we do not see an enlarged object, but an image of it. The image is real and according to quality of lens used, a more or less perfect representation on a much larger scale of the object itself.

C

In a hand lens or magnifying glass there is no real image, as we see the object itself, but the lens changing the direction of the light rays from object to eye, causes the eye to perceive them as though the rays came from a larger object, and every part of the object becomes to our perceptions as though it were enlarged accordingly. (Fig. 25.)

CHAPTER IV.

ACHROMATISM.

Objective lenses.—Light is of composite character, being a mixture of various colours whose effect when the eye sees them simultaneously is white. When a lens refracts or bends the rays it does not bend all the coloured rays equally, hence a common or single lens gives a fringe of colour all round the object. By suitably arranging two lenses of different form and density, however, any two colours can be made to combine by being superposed on each other. Two colours are selected which are so bright visually that the outstanding faint image of the duller colours are practically suppressed by contrast. The lens thus made is said

Fig. 26.—Low Power Objective Lens.

to be " achromatic," and it is only for the highest powers and the most delicate tests that anything more optically perfect is required. It is possible, however, by a more complicated arrangement of materials of differing density (or, as it is called, " index of refraction "), to bring three bright colours into superposition when the lens is said to be " apochromatic," but the

character of these lenses had better be studied when
such advanced work is reached that they become desirable. They are difficult to use by the beginner as they
need special eyepieces, which need adjustment in use,
and it requires a trained eye to judge the precision
necessary to induce their superior performance. The
effect of perfect combination of all the colours is
reached, however, by the aid of the eyepiece in addition to the objective, as although three colours are
brought to a focus in one plane by the so-called apochromatic objective they are not all of one size and the
adjustment needed is that of an eyepiece having dif-

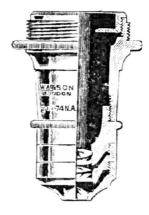

Fig. 27.—High Power Objective.

ferent magnifications for various colours, and this is so
adjusted in use that the images are made to appear
coincident, and thus render the lens apochromatic, but
the term should rather be applied to the whole microscope tube so fitted as neither lens is truly apochromatic used alone. The combination of objective and
eyepiece form an apochromatic system. Good achromatic objectives are now to be purchased at a reasonable price, which are of such perfection that a microscopist might work for years and never need nor hope
for anything better, and many good workers have never

even seen the superior type, so they are by no means essential for a beginner.

An intermediate type is called semi-apochromatic and possesses some of the characters of either type. These are turned out at an intermediate price by all the best makers, but the achromatic form will answer every call made on them and will suffice for all but the master.

An objective lens on a modern microscope consists of several lenses placed in a brass mount, each of which performs some function in removing the imperfections which would exist in the resultant image if the whole work were done by one lens made of one kind of glass only

The serious student or the really advanced microscopist would do well to learn the whole theory underlying the reasons for several glasses being necessary, but the beginner had better regard the whole combination as one lens, and treat it as one lens which is the equivalent of the several which are doing the whole of the work. The only thing to notice is that the nominal focus does not give the frontal distance of lens to object, because the refraction as a whole being the result of several lenses the focus is reckoned as though an equivalent lens did it all.

As, however, it is done by more than one, placed behind each other, the centre of work is between the lenses, and if one alone were doing it all it would be farther back, hence the frontal distance is always less than the nominal focus

The distance from front of lens to object in a really good inch lens is seldom more than $\frac{2}{3}$ of an inch, and this is called the working distance. It must further be observed that it is not usual for makers to give the equivalent focus of lenses but to name them according to their initial magnification of a ten-inch tube, without counting the magnification of the eyepiece lens

CHAPTER V.

MAGNIFICATION.

An eyepiece magnifying five times on a ten-inch tube with a lens called a " one-inch objective " gives a linear magnification of 50 times. An objective of this power is called a one-inch lens, which is not quite correct, but it is the conventional method of expressing its power. The same lens used on a tube 6½ inches long, which is the length now more general, and with the same eyepiece, gives a magnification of 37½ diameters, because in a 6½-inch tube the image formed and intercepted as it were by the eyepiece is smaller than it would be if it had been allowed to form and be focussed at ten inches

Initial magnification depends on the proportion between the relative distance of the formed image to optical centre of lens bears to the distance of optical centre of lens to the object. This image is magnified by the eyepiece, the magnification of each eyepiece being a fixed quantity whatever the length of tube The image being larger and farther away it is from the objective lens it is formed, the total magnification is that of the larger image magnified by the constant eyepiece.

The lenses hitherto spoken of, and to which the beginner is recommended for the first few months to confine himself, are all " dry " lenses; that is, there is air between the object and the front of lens

There is, however, a type of lens in use for high power called " immersion." These differ from others

in the fact that a film of fluid is interposed between
the front of lens and the object, the fluid being as near
as possible of the same refractive index as glass. They
are of two kinds: water immersion and oil immersion.
The use of the first type is confined principally to the
examination of objects living in water, so that the
lens front is actually immersed in the water in which
the living objects are. The second type, the " oil immersion," has for its *raison d'être*, firstly the increased
light got by avoiding reflected light at very oblique
angles not entering the lens owing to its great obliquity,

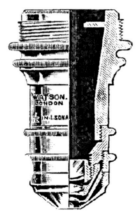

Fig. 28.—Oil Immersion Objective.

causing the light from the cover glass to be refracted
out of the field of the lens. Secondly, that the oil used
for immersing the front of the lens being of the same
and similar refractive index as glass, the thickness of
the glass cover becomes a negligible quantity, as the
substance between the actual object and lens being
homogeneous throughout the thickness of either is
immaterial. The gain in actual working aperture of a
lens almost touching, such as 1/12 inch, is equal to
almost half as much again in the quantity of light
passed. As working aperture also affects resolution,

about forty per cent. more is gained in defining power.
The oil is applied with a little rod, usually a continua-
tion of the stopper, and a very small quantity should
be placed as a hanging drop on the lens front, which
should afterwards be lowered into place and focus.
The beginner is earnestly advised to leave them
severely alone until such time as he requires a more
advanced book than this professes to be; and, unless
already in an outfit, by no means to purchase one

Correction collar —A ring with milled edge, capable
of being rotated, called a correction collar is sometimes fitted to an objective lens; it enables the interior
pair of the combination to be brought nearer to the
front glass, or farther away from it   This is to
ensure the performance of the lens at its very best
when the arrangement is upset by the object being
covered with a glass thicker or thinner than the
optician's computations has provided for   It is not
necessary with the lower powers as the disturbance
caused by varying thickness of cover glass is negligible,
but for higher powers used dry it is really required for
perfection of image unless the object is covered with
glass of a specified thickness anticipated by the
optician who calculated the lens   Figures and a mark
will be found on the mount when a correction collar is
provided, and the numbers usually refer to the number
of thousandths of an inch the cover glass should be for
the lens to perform best at the mark.

At the commencement of microscopic work the
existence of the correction collar can be ignored and
the collar left in its middle position, but after experience has been gained it will be found that on every
mounted object there is a position of the collar where
the lens defines better than elsewhere, but the superio-
rity is not marked till the eye has been trained by
practice to recognise it.

The eyepiece or ocular.—This is the lens dropped

into top of draw tube which collects light from the objective lens and resolves it into an enlarged image of the object. In its almost universal use for the microscope, it consists of two lenses placed with their convex sides downwards; the lower of which, called the field lens, condenses the light and brings the image into the field of view of the eye lens, which is the top lens, so that it can be received by the eye. As these

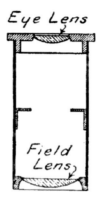

Fig. 29.—The Eye-piece.

lenses are placed at such a distance apart that its focus lies between or within the lenses and has no positive focus outside, it is called a negative lens.

There are other eyepieces occasionally used for special purposes, such as measuring, etc., but being only used for these special objects, need not be regarded by the beginner. The lens above, called the " Huyghenian," to distinguish it from other forms of eyepiece, is made in various powers to magnify anything from three to about 27 diameters. It is seldom engraved with its magnifying power, although there is a growing tendency amongst opticians to do so, it being usually marked A, B, C, etc., which give successively about four times, six times, or eight times in magnification of the image.   The lower magnifications, such as A, B, or C, are the best to use, as the lowest gives more light and the eye does not need to be so close to the eye lens in use.

The eyepiece is made in various sizes to fit the varying diameters of draw tube in use, but the size in most general use for all but the most expensive type of microscope is the R M.S. No. 1 size, which drops into a tube of .9173 inch diameter inside

This is the cheapest size to buy, the various powers costing about five shillings each new.   The larger sizes cost more, rising with diameter.

CHAPTER VI.

ILLUMINATION.

The " Bull's Eye."—This piece of apparatus is used for arranging the light from lamp into a convenient form for illuminating the object. Should the object be opaque, such as seeds, tiny shells, or any object mounted on a black background, the illuminant should be placed above the level of the stage and the light

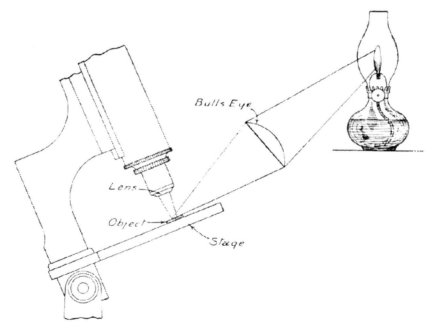

Fig. 30.—Lighting Opaque Objects.

from it focussed on to the object by the bull's eye. The aim is to get the smallest and brightest image of the flame focussed exactly on the object under examination, so that the light reflected from the object is gathered up by the lens to form an image. It is important to observe that if the flame be distant from the microscope stage, the convex side of " bull's eye " should be turned towards the light, as the errors due to the lens being single and uncorrected are less when used that way. The flat side of " bull's eye " should always be facing the shorter focus.

This piece of apparatus can also be used to focus a thin flat beam of light sideways across an object. This is managed by placing the light very slightly above the stage and the " bull's eye " in between with convex side downwards. The light from lamp strikes

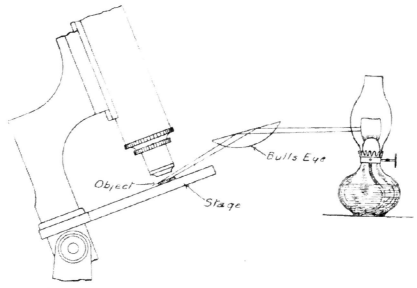

Fig. 31.　Lighting Opaque Objects with Short Focus Objective.

the convex side of " bull's eye," is refracted, and reaches the flat side at such an angle of obliquity that it is totally reflected and emerges in the form of a thin flat feather which can pass under the front of lens and yet give a strong side-light on the object. Of course, this illumination is very one-sided and causes deep shadows, but with opaque objects it is a good

way of looking at them if short focus lenses are in
use and where there is no room for any other method
of lighting them.   (Fig. 31.)

The purpose for which the " bull's-eye " is oftenest
used, however, is to get parallel light from a divergent source, or to collect all the divergent rays from
a lamp that can be collected and turn them in a

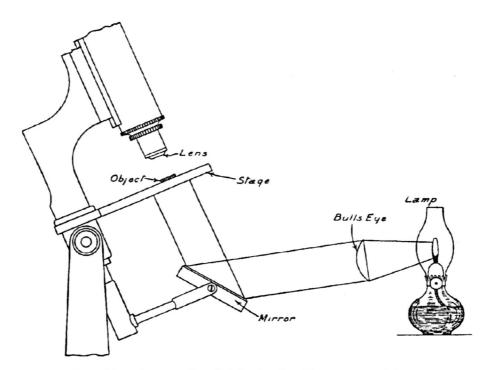

Fig. 32.—Getting Parallel Light for Transparent Objects
by means of the Bull's Eye.

parallel beam on to the mirror of the microscope,
whence they can be turned into optic axis and used
as desired   To this end the *flat* side of condenser is
turned towards source of light and the " bull's eye "
collects all rays diverging from lamp and, if properly
placed at the right distance, the emergent beam is
approximately parallel.   There is no contradiction in

turning flat side to light as the shortest focus in this
case *is* toward the lamp. The way to test whether
the " bull's eye " is the right distance from lamp is
proved by receiving an image of the lamp flame on a
card and this image should not change greatly in size
when card is moved nearer to or farther from " bull's
eye." If card be removed further from lamp and the
image grows larger, put " bull's eye " a trifle nearer
to lamp flame; if the image tends to get smaller as
card is removed farther away, increase slightly distance
between " bull's eye " and lamp. For the initial
trials it may be mentioned that the smaller and usual
sizes of " bull's eye " require to be placed about three
inches from lamp flame. It is rather important to get
this adjustment right. It is often done anyhow as
long as the object is lit, but in getting critical illumination for difficult objects, or getting good dark ground
illumination of an object, it is *essential* that it be correct   The habit of adjusting this simple piece of
apparatus once correctly acquired, removes a lot of
difficulty in getting effects otherwise troublesome to
obtain   Condensers are calculated by opticians to
receive parallel light and if convergent or divergent
light is supplied the perfection intended by the maker
is not obtained, as it may not be possible to focus
condenser properly to compensate for the wrong conditions. Divergent light can be focussed by lowering
the condenser further away from the slide, convergent
light by raising the condenser toward the slide   In
the latter case it may be that the front of condenser
will lift up the slide whilst trying to reach the focus,
which will be so short as to be within the slide itself
and perfect position unobtainable.

Silver side reflector —For the illumination from
above of opaque objects, in addition to a bull's eye,
there is used a silver side reflector, or a concave silver
reflector fitted on the lens. The side reflector is

made to a parabolic curve so that parallel rays of light from the bull's eye falling on the reflector are condensed to a point of light on the object if the position of reflector is properly arranged. The light from lamp,

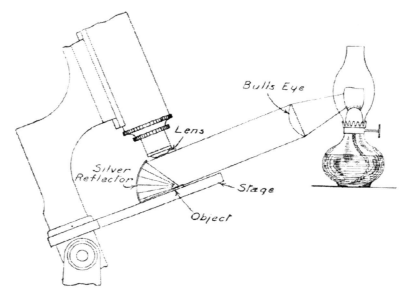

Fig. 33.—Using the Silver Side Reflector for Opaque Objects.

which should be somewhat above the object and about eight inches distant, is received and made parallel by a bull's eye so that it falls into the reflector and is returned to the focus of the reflector exactly on the

Fig. 34.—Silver Side Reflector.

object. The condition desirable is that a small point should be formed on the object, and further that a small amount of the parallel light should cross this spot in order that the illumination should not be altogether one-sided. This is arranged by trial and error till the brightest and best result is obtained. It can then be focussed and the illuminating arrangement can remain whilst other specimens are examined, as it will not usually need further attention. (Figs 33 and 34.)

A "Lieberkohn" is a concave silver reflector fixed on the lens to receive light from the mirror, passing the sides of the object which is fixed on a transparent slide, the light being reflected and cast down into the centre of the field of view. As these reflectors have to agree with the focus of objective lens a separate one is required for each lens

These pieces of apparatus are of course only suitable for the lower powers They are both desirable and useful to examine external appearance, but it is impossible to light an object with them when the lens approaches very closely to it. Internal structure and very fine detail must be studied by preparing the object and rendering it transparent, which is treated of later on.

The beginner will not find the reflectors absolutely indispensable, as very good lighting can be got without incurring the expense of purchasing them

CHAPTER VII.

ACCESSORIES

The polariscope.—It is quite impossible in the space available to enter into any descriptive theory of the polarisation of light It must suffice to explain that light, after passing through a piece of Iceland spar, which has been cut in certain directions, polished and mounted, possesses a character somewhat different to ordinary light Shortly, instead of the light vibrations being in all directions, the light after passing through the prism only vibrates in one plane as though it had been passed through something like the bars of a grid-iron, which only allowed it to go straight up and down. If now a piece of this spar, called a polariser, is fitted under the microscope stage, and another piece, called the analyser, is mounted behind the objective lens, any object on the stage can be examined whilst one of these pieces is rotated Usually the part beneath the stage is the rotating prism With suitable objects a fine play of colours is produced by rotating the prism, and if a thin plate of mica or selenite be placed beneath the object slide, the gorgeous colours changing with every slight movement of the polarising prism is something quite wonderful to behold. The colours vary according to the thickness of the selenite film, and these latter can be purchased of differing kinds to show different colour predominance. The most suitable objects for polariscopic beauty are thin slices of stone or rock, horn crystals, some insects, fish scales, cotton threads, fine grains of sand, etc. The easiest to get are crystals of most chemical salts

dissolved in water and dried on the slide. This will
be referred to in slide making. As a means of enjoyment and interesting one's friends, a polariscope
attachment is a most desirable accessory which will
do more to provide an enjoyable entertainment at any
time than any amount of magnification will do without
one.

It is with this piece of apparatus that the writer
has found the use of the incandescent gas lamp so
beneficial, as much light incident on the prisms is not
passed through them. The polariser splits the inci-

Fig. 35.——Polariser.   Analyser.   Cover.

dent light into two, each ray being divided. One of
these called the ordinary and the other the extraordi-
nary ray. As one of these is thrown right out of the
field of view only half of the original light can reach
the object. The analysing prism behaves to the light
in exactly the same way, dividing the light reaching it
into two, only half of which can pass to form an
image. Hence without any absorption by the object,
one quarter of the original light at most can reach the
eye.

The white colour of incandescent gas as compared
with the yellow light of a comparatively feeble oil
lamp further accentuates the advantage, and a gem
burner of about 30 candle power, as against an oil
lamp of about seven, gives wonderfully enhanced

brilliancy to the polariscope. When the light passed by the polarising prism impinges upon any substance capable of double refraction, the light is again split into rays which do not follow exactly the same course. It is the interference of these divided rays with each other which cause the brilliant colour effects shown by the polariscope When crests of a light wave of any one colour are superposed upon crests of another light wave of the same colour the amplitude of the wave is doubled and the colour enhanced accordingly. When crests of light waves, instead of being superposed on crests, are so disposed by retardation of either ray in phase as to correspond with depressions of the same colour, that colour is extinguished. It so happens that the extinction of one colour at one portion of the revolution times with the doubling of other colours, and the changes of hue or colour seen on the same object are accounted for The complete understanding of this subject does not belong to elementary microscopy, but this is as simple an explanation of the phenomena as can be given.

The erector —This is an instrument little used. Its function is to reverse the inverted to an upright image by a second reversal within the microscope tube. It is exactly similar on a smaller scale to the erector found in telescopes used for terrestrial purposes. It consists of two lenses at suitable distances apart mounted in a tube which screws or slides into the lower end of the draw tube. Theoretically, it should upset the computations of the optician in forming a well corrected objective lens, but the lower powers of the microscope will stand a good bit of variation without perceptible loss of definition, and, although it is not worth buying, if one should be in the outfit it may be used for dissecting purposes, or for mounting in arranging objects on the slide, or for removing the undesirable particles that seem to have a most objectionable habit of getting into a mount even when clean working has been attained.

There are two lenses in a tube about three inches long with the power of refracting the light sufficiently to cause the rays to cross in a diaphragm placed between them. This again inverts the image and causes it to appear to the eye in the same position as the object lies on the stage. When present in a microscope it causes the effect of the draw tube to be much greater in varying magnification of an object, but it is not the best way to effect variable magnification, there being a distinct loss of light and defining power. It should only be used to work upon objects under treatment by instruments in the hands. It is better, however, to learn the manipulation of objects on the stage in their inverted order by a little practice, where it becomes so much a habit that the presence of an erector is a distinct hindrance, the writer finding it so when one of the opticians was showing him a new form of this piece of apparatus. He was quite unable to get the object correctly placed without assistance.

CHAPTER VIII

CHOOSING A MICROSCOPE

Choosing a microscope —The best way to procure a good instrument is undoubtedly to pay the best price and put yourself in the hands of the best opticians, but this method is prohibitive to many who do know the points of a good microscope, and usually impossible to the beginner who desires to start as a rule without incurring too large an expenditure.

Unfortunately, the market is flooded with a lot of cheap and nasty instruments of undecided origin These are sold in polished cases containing a few useful accessories and a fearful and wonderful assortment of things seldom wanted. This is usually described as a complete outfit and is made to no design or standard. If one already possesses such an instrument the best possible use must be made of it. If, however, a new microscope is to be procured, it is best to get a plain one from any leading optician, which will be made to standard sizes and fittings. Then as progress is made, new additions may be added as required with the certainty of them fitting All the best makers now offer such an instrument, which costs no more than the pawnbroker's " box of tricks " made by nobody in particular, and for which nobody is responsible. Standard fittings by standard makers are all interchangeable, and the English makers, I think, cater best for the plain standard microscope suitable for further additions. If new, begin with one eyepiece and that a low power, not magnifying more than four or five times, and if only one objective can be purchased get the " one-inch," which is the most generally useful and more often used than any other. If two can be obtained, get the " one-" and the " two-inch," leaving higher power severely alone till skill in the use of these has been attained and the necessity of higher magnification clearly felt. Avoid " button " lenses and dividing ones, as a good inch by a first rate maker will show all that the highest power of a dividing combination with low aperture can show. A maker cannot correct lenses for the various aberrations, each perfect and complete in itself, and yet perfect in combination, and any attempt to do so sacrifices something of perfection somewhere Get a plain non-dividing lens as good as possible at its computed best and leave it at that, as some good point must be given up in combination lenses Do not be misled by too much polish and show A microscope is to look through, not at, a means to an end, not an end in itself It may be an ornament, but its main duty is to serve a use Messrs. Angus, of Wigmore Street; Baker, of Holborn; and Watson, of Holborn, all issue secondhand lists and only deal in reasonably good class apparatus, and as they have a reputation to conserve the beginner is quite safe in their hands without expert assistance, and the price asked is not more than equal quality goods elsewhere. If purchasing secondhand from a stranger get a microscopist's advice where possible, and if it cannot be obtained look specially at the following points, as a bad lens can be replaced separately, but a bad stand means a useless instrument.

If one has the power of choice do not, by any means, get a microscope that cannot be inclined from the vertical. There are some instruments on the market very good in character which are very inconvenient for prolonged use. It is well to be able to place the instrument vertically when examining water in dishes or trays, but when the eye is looking vertically down it means a standing position all the time, and occasionally the fluid on the eye will impair good definition if used constantly for any length of time in this position. Sitting down is far more comfortable if much seeing is to be done.

The microscope chosen should be of recent type, and bear a maker's name, should stand steady on its base, and not be easily overturned   The hinge joint for inclining should work freely, yet remain steady when using the other adjustments.   The coarse focussing should move smoothly without backlash or lost motion in turning handles and not stiffly.   The slides should work without the slightest shake, and if there is no means of adjusting them, the slightest looseness should condemn the instrument

The same smoothness and absence of backlash or lost motion must be looked for in the fine adjustment, but all the modern microscopes have means of compensating for wear in the slides by tightening a screw or two.   Avoid the microscopes which have a fine adjustment by means of an inner tube holding the objective, which is worked through a slot in the tube They always work loose after a little wear and the image is displaced by its rocking from side to side when used

If fitted with a focussing substage, test the slides of that in the same way, and a smooth easy movement should be looked for or the cost of professional overhauling and adjustment allowed for.

In looking through the lenses, any fine object bearing thin hairs is a good rough test, and the image should be free from colour fringes and define cleanly and sharply   It is almost impossible to tell a beginner how to judge a lens, so none which do not bear a maker's name should be allowed for in bargaining. See that the thread of lenses is to standard—36 threads 4/5th inch outside, there are a lot of ancient lenses about which require adapters, being much smaller, and to get an adapter cut is troublesome.　The standard eyepieces run: No. 1, .9173; No. 2, 1.04; No 3, 1.27, No. 4, 1.41 inches in diameter, but a poor eyepiece need not deter if stand is good, as they are not outrageously expensive. Any microscope really modern will be one of these sizes.

CHAPTER IX

USING A MICROSCOPE

Using the microscope —The first word should be to take exact notice of the microscope in its case before unpacking it, and observe exactly how it is stowed away, noticing the arrangement of all the parts whose uses have been previously described. This is a very necessary word of warning, as the makers, to get cases for transport as small as they conveniently can, get the instrument into its smallest compass, and if in putting it back the arrangement as to inclination and disposition of parts is not just the same as before withdrawal it will be very difficult to ensure replacement in the case without strain or damage. A little forethought in this direction will be well repaid when it is put back.

The instrument, being taken from its case, should preferably be placed in a tray on the table, the smaller end of the tray being toward the operator. This is better than on the table direct, because if it be desired to shew the microscope to others after the lighting is all well arranged, the whole tray, lamp, etc., can be pushed across to other observers without disturbing any arrangements that have been made, and the only alteration required will be the adjustment of focus necessary to accommodate the eyes of differing persons, which, of course, varies according to their usual sight

It will be better also than placed on the usual tablecloth, as if oil be spilled from lamp, or water from specimens a tray is more easily cleaned than a cloth

The microscope should be arranged with its back leg, or back of stand, nearest the edge of tray, and, if daylight be used, in front of a window facing away from the sun. Let it be sloped to comfortably afford a view through the tube when sitter is in a convenient position A low power, say " one " or " two " inch objective lens, should be screwed into nose-piece, and the eyepiece dropped into top of tube When working by daylight and without a condenser, the concave mirror will be found to be the best. This should be turned so that its centre is exactly opposite a continued line drawn through the main tube downwards, as if much out of centre the image will seem to move when it is focussed.

The gimbal holding the mirror should be placed horizontally and then, the eye looking down the tube, the mirror should be rocked on its axis points till the field is full of light. Should there be found any difficulty from the description given to get the light into the field, it might be found useful to practise for a few minutes at finding the light by looking down the tube with both eyepiece and objective removed

On looking down the tube the mirror will be seen, but not very brightly. Placing both arms on the table, one at each side of the microscope, and resting the wrists on tray or table, with thumb and first fingers of each hand take hold of rim of mirror and tilt it till the light is reflected direct to the eye. If this does not happen with first trial gently rock the mirror on its pivot whilst tilting it, and the light will soon come into view. Practise this by throwing it out of place and finding it again a few times, then replace the lenses, and the little lesson will have been learnt for always and the few minutes well spent These little tricks of usage soon become natural, and one wonders how ever there was a difficulty about it.

A prepared mount should now be taken of a transparent character in which the object selected is fairly large This can be roughly focussed after placing it under the slips, the plain side of glass slip, of course, to be in contact with the stage. To focus it is well to begin by racking the tube down almost to the glass without looking through the eyepiece, placing the front of objective lens, say, $\frac{1}{4}$ inch from the slide. Then, whilst looking through the eyepiece, carefully and somewhat slowly raise the tube until the image comes into view. As it resolves itself into an enlarged image of the object, move more slowly and more carefully till it begins to lose again a shade. You have then passed the proper focus and must rack down, feeling your way until the utmost sharpness and clearness is obtained Do not use the fine adjustment for low powers, as it is desirable at first to cultivate a delicate touch on the coarse motions Do not bear on the milled heads when turning them, but learn to twist them quite slowly and evenly without strain on the spindle at all. The object will now probably be in sight. but not well or centrally arranged in the field of view, and the first difficulty is now met, because any attempt to arrange it only displaces it further It is inverted, and as the few words on " an image " shews, the motions for arranging it must be reversed Now this reversed motion *must* be learnt, and learnt so thoroughly that by practice it becomes second nature. It is easy to arrange the large object because it may not go entirely off the field when pushed in the wrong direction (which, of course, the tyro feels is the right one), but when smaller objects are looked at, a slight movement in the wrong direction will take them right out of sight and it may be a long time before it is found again. The reversing movement once thoroughly acquired and made, as it were, a part of one's self, a mechanical stage is looked upon as quite an undesirable acquisition. The object being centred as well as you can, it will now in all probability be found that other things are in the field of view These may be specks of dirt, cloudiness, windows bars focussed on the object, or unequal illumination from passing clouds. If specks of dirt are in the field of view, their cause must be sought for in this way. First revolve the eyepiece in the tube and see if specks revolve with it. If they do, they may be caused by small particles on the inside of the lenses. The lenses must be unscrewed carefully one at a time, the open end from which lens has been removed being placed downwards on the tray whilst lens is cleaned with a very soft piece of clean fine linen or chamois leather It must not be rubbed hard, but gently wiped with a twisting motion. When one is cleaned replace it, making quite sure that the fine threads are not crossed. They screw in quite easily and without the slightest force if started right. Then drop the eyepiece in place and look if specks are gone If not, remove the other lens at opposite end of eyepiece and clean it also If both lenses of an eyepiece are clean there will be no dirt visible which moves around when the lens is rotated in the tube. If there be dirt which does not move with eyepiece, next try the slide and clean it both sides carefully It can be told easily if it be on the slide, as if the slide is moved the dirt on it moves with it The eyepiece and slide being clean, if there still be specks, slightly tilt the mirror, as anything on the mirror may show on the image If the dirt moves with a slight movement of mirror, the mirror must be cleaned If there be, after all this, still a piece of dirt, it must be on the objective lens This should always be left till last, as the less the objective is cleaned the better. Being kept in brass boxes there is not much chance of dirt getting on them, so when putting microscope away if we clean the objective on the nosepiece, leave the eyepiece also in the tube. Dirt will hardly lodge on the lower glass as it faces downwards, the upper, if dirty, should be carefully brushed with a soft camel hair brush. It is strongly advised that an objective lens should never under any circumstances be unscrewed by a beginner. It is better to put up with a little dirt till you meet a friend who knows how to remove it properly or send it to an optician Objectives are so adjusted that if not arranged exactly as the maker intended, their perform-ance is very much impaired. It may be well to men-tion here that an objective should never be screwed into its place carelessly with one hand only. The other hand should support it in case of a slip, as if dropped on the stage the front glass may be chipped and ruined irretrievably, and in the higher powers the front glass might be knocked in from its seating. A little care saves a nasty smash, and if the operation is performed rightly at first one does not do it wrongly another time.

Sometimes in getting the field of view well illumi-nated, difficulty may be experienced by the microscope being too much inclined, and the mirror having to be placed so obliquely to the light that its projection is too narrow an ellipse. This is shewn when it is im-possible to get both top and bottom of the field well lit at one time, the rim of mirror coming into the field at one or the other place in turn   The obvious remedy for this is to place the instrument more nearly vertical or raise the light. Placing the instrument nearer the vertical is the better method, as otherwise the direct glare from lamp into the observing eye may disturb its powers of regarding the image.

It will sometimes happen with daylight from a window that images of window bars or image of cur-tains before a window are visible as well as the object. Should this be so, try slightly moving the microscope to get a clear image of the sky only, and if this be impossible, try altering the height of mirror by sliding it up and down the tail rod. An evenly lit field of view is desirable for low powers and is much more comfortable to look at, but to get the best out of higher powers " critical illumination " is necessary, and is treated of elsewhere. Critical illumination, however, is not essential for the general run of beginner's work, and at the commencement he will consider the evenly lighted field preferable.

Cultivate from the beginning the use of either eye, as both want training in observation, and if many slides in succession are examined for any length of time the relief of using either eye will be appreciated. It is not necessary to close the eye not in use as the

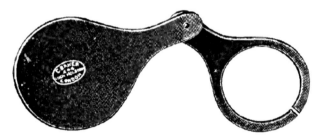

Fig. 36.——Eyeshade.

brain can, with a little practice, ignore the image seen by the eye not looking down the tube. There is a little rearrangement made to rest on the top of microscope to shade the eye not in use. (Fig. 36.)

This consists of two parts, as figured, jointed in the middle; one part has in it a circular aperture which slides over the draw-tube of the microscope, and the other part shuts out the light from the disengaged eye when using a monocular microscope. It is made in vulcanite.

It is always advisable with low powers to close in the iris diaphragm beneath the stage a little from its largest aperture. There is no advantage in passing a larger bundle of light than the object in the field of

view requires when no substage condenser is in use
Any light not required only causes glare and detracts
from the brilliancy of the desired image. Most microscopical amateurs who have to work for a living have
only the evenings free for their hobby, and artificial
light then becomes necessary. It is much more under
control, and its point of origin being at hand can be
arranged to one's own desires. Daylight being diffuse,
cannot be regulated with the same precision as artificial light, and if a bull's-eye be placed at the proper
distance from the lamp a bundle of parallel rays can
be obtained. If artificial light is used arrange the
microscope in tray as described on a previous page,
and place the lamp at back of tray about eight inches
from the instrument in front with the flame as low
down as convenient. For an evenly lighted field and
low power lens the broad side of flame should face
the mirror. The bull's-eye can now be placed about
three inches from the flame, and in the path of direct
rays from flame to mirror. The mirror should then be
arranged as for daylight by tilting till field of view is
well and evenly lit. It should appear as a bright disc
equally illuminated all over, if not, shift carefully
distance of bull's-eye from lamp, or alter the height
of bull's-eye till all is as desired. The object can then
be treated for focus, etc., as for daylight. After once
arranging the apparatus in the tray another slide can
be inserted as desired, only a slight touch of the focussing handle being required to sharpen it up to compensate for varying distance from lens, owing to
different thicknesses of glass slides.

Arranged as described, there will, with flat, thin,
transparent slides, be rather too much light, so that
the eye is tired quickly. This can be reduced, in great
measure, by closing the diaphragm beneath the stage,
thus limiting the amount of light available. Should it
be necessary to close the orifice to such a small one

that the definition of the image falls away, before
reducing the intensity of the light sufficiently, it would
be better to interpose a screen to cut down the light,
than to reduce the diaphragm to a pinhole.   Most
microscope lamps have tinted glasses on chimneys
available, and the faint blue glass will generally be
sufficient to reduce the light, if too intense   This also
has the further advantage that it cuts off the yellow
colour, so characteristic of an oil lamp light, and the
object is then shown more nearly in it proper colours.
It is more restful to the eye to have plenty of light
of the right kind, than too little of the wrong   There
are various means of interposing the bluish screen : A
circle to lie in the bull's-eye; an extra glass for the
lamp; a separate glass or trough mounted similar to a
bull's-eye; or the ring fitting, which is usually fitted
beneath the stage, and for which all the best opticians
keep various light modifiers of coloured glass or ground
glass.   The ring attached to the iris diaphragm is in
practice as good a place as any, as the glass discs are
so easily and quickly changed, without deranging any
other adjustment.   Sometimes the removal of the
bull's-eye will do all that is required to reduce the
illumination, but practical workers almost invariably
prefer to work with parallel rather than divergent light.

We have hitherto regarded the microscope as though
it were always used to observe transparent objects, and
the majority of prepared specimens are so finished.
There are, however, many that can only be seen properly by reflected light, and the mode of lighting them
will now be described.

The external character of objects, rather than their
internal, often gives a better idea of their general
nature; and as is remarked elsewhere, there need be
no lack of objects anywhere, even if there be a lack
of prepared slides

The microscope is placed as before in front and the

light raised well above the level of the stage with the bull's-eye more distant from the light and at its focus from the object on the stage. It should be so placed that an image of the light as almost a point is made to converge on the slide exactly in the centre of the field of view. If the light be very close to the microscope stage it will be impossible to focus an image of the flame upon the object by means of the bull's-eye condenser This distance will depend on the focus of the bull's-eye, and the image of the flame upon the object is smaller the farther the light is removed from the microscope If there be a good incandescent gas-burner overhead, very good results can be got from that alone with powers up to an inch If, however, any power higher than an inch is in use, the lens mount will be so near the object that it will be in the way of condensing the light in the right place by the direct method. A little practice with a white card in the left hand and the bull's-eye in the right, and trying to get the brightest and smallest focus of the light on the card will soon show the principle involved without necessarily learning the theory of it. Most persons have tried at some time or other to set fire to a card with a lens as a " burning glass," and the same method of getting the spot of light on the object, as boys used to get an image of the sun on a card, will suffice to get an opaque object well illuminated by top light. The only thing to notice is that the source of light being nearer than the sun, the focus of the lens will seem longer

Be careful to turn the convex side of bull's-eye to the light in this case This form of illumination is brilliant, but one-sided, but unless the object be very deep the shadows cast will not be disturbing If, however, a side silver reflector be possessed and used the lighting is still brighter, and a little of the direct light, with management, can be arranged to illuminate the

F

shadow side.   Of course, this cannot well be done from an overhead light, but can be arranged very nicely by having the lamp about ten inches distant and above the level of the stage

To get illumination on an opaque object when a lens of higher than one inch is used the method described under " Bull's-eye " of getting a thin feather or flat beam of light under the objective may be tried. This being oblique casts rather severe shadows, but as any object requiring a high power must be thin this need not detract from its use.

Critical illumination.—Critical illumination is a term used to express a condition existing when the arrangement of light is such that the highest and best resolution of an objective lens can be obtained.   The beginner really does not require the condition as it is usually an unevenly lit field, and his earlier endeavours had better be devoted to learning everything possible refer to it at all for a beginner except that he must learn to get critical lighting as a means of getting dark ground illumination satisfactorily. If he knows how to get it, when required, he can always get the popular bright image on a dark field   The means of attaining the desired result essentially consists of a condenser beneath the stage, accurately central and accurately focussed.   This exactly produces a tiny brilliant image of the light on the object, the object itself being in the focus of the objective lens.   Both must be in focus at one time, and both must be in the same central line   With a lamp the result is a bright streak of light vertically formed across the field, and the object is, if necessary, observed a bit at a time by passing it through the brilliant narrow streak, which is the exact image of the lamp flame, and for which the edge of flame is presented to the mirror.

To get this form of image one must proceed as follows   Place the microscope and lamp in tray with

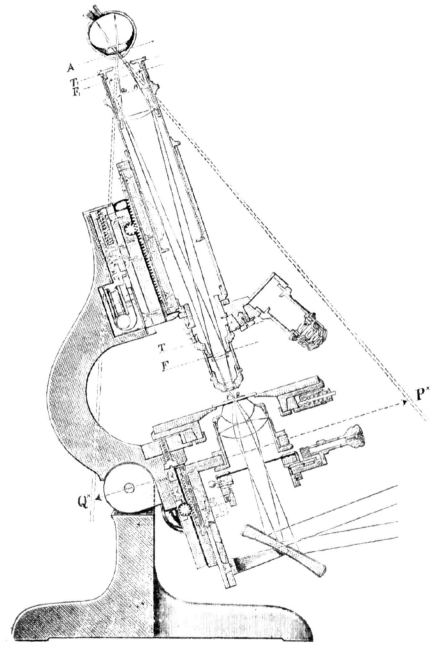

Fig. 37. Course of Light Rays in "Critical" Illumination.

the edge of flame towards the instrument and get as
good a lit field as one can. Then, closing in the iris
diaphragm to its smallest orifice, and with the condenser in place, with a low power lens see if the small
picture of the hole is in the centre of the field of view,
If it be, all well and good; but if not, and there are
centering screws to the substage, adjust them by turning until the image of the hole is in the centre. If no
centering screws, and the condenser is in an understage
sleeved fitting, it will usually be found that a partial
rotation of condenser in its sleeve will accomplish the
end in view. At any rate, get is as central as possible,
and leave as little as possible to be arranged by moving
the mirror or slightly shifting the lamp, both of which
means may be used to obviate trifling errors of cen-
trality. Then getting a glass slip on the stage and
opening the diaphragm, focus with the object on it,
and when this is sharp rack the substage condenser up
and down till the image of the flame is exactly in focus
also   The objective lens it is desired to use, can now
be substituted, and the image of flame, instead of being
small in the centre of the field, will be spread right
across it, or will do so when diaphragm is opened out
fully. The top lens of condenser will usually be found
to be almost in contact with underside of slide when
in correct focus. Should it be impossible to raise up
condenser sufficiently to get into focus without it
touching and raising the slide, the lamp should be
brought nearer the mirror, as this increases the upper
conjugate focus of lens, and allows it to be longer.
You now have critical light, and if you desire the flame
to be more evenly distributed over the field of view
the lamp may be rotated to get the broad side in place
of the edge into play; or the condenser may be dropped
a trifle to spread the cone of light, or rather to take it
at a lower point than the apex of the cone, and you
will get an evenly lighted field. This, however will *not*

be " critical illumination," but will serve for almost every purpose for which a microscope can be used. There are even among experts different opinions as to the critical use of the light, but no difference of opinion that all microscopists should know how to get it.

The evenly lit field can also be got by focussing on a bull's-eye placed with flat side to lamp and treating the bull's-eye full of light as the illuminant itself, and this method is in more general use than any for ordinary observations. The bull's-eye must be its exact focal distance from lamp, which can be tested by receiving the image of lamp flame on a card. If bull's-eye is right distance from lamp the image formed on card by the lamp flame will be the same size at any distance of card, as previously remarked. This can be tried for the bull's-eye separately and the distance noted once for all. A ground glass disc is sometimes used to diffuse the light but, in the writer's experience, the performance of any lens is inferior when used thus. If ground glass must be used it should be near the light and accurately focussed on the slide, the brightly illuminated ground glass being treated as though it were self-luminous, every point of its surface being a point of illumination, with its opposite conjugate focus on the object This can easily be arranged by having two glasses, both ground, one of which has been ruled with fine lines with black ink. This is focussed as for critical illumination When correct focus is found, the glasses are changed, the plain ground glass being put where the ruled one was, being careful to see it is the same way round The glass itself is then in exact focus, and critical illumination and an evenly lit field are both obtained at once

The proper use of the lamp is of great importance if oil be used The budding microscopist will not be popular with the rest of the household if he, by carelessness or laziness, indulges his hobby by means of an evil smelling lamp. The burner should be periodically cleaned, and at all times any oil spilled on the reservoir of lamp or its burner, removed before lighting it. To get a good light the burner should be slowly turned up as far as it will go to just smoke, and then lowered just far enough to stop the smoking. By this means the maximum brilliancy of the particular lamp can be reached. To whiten the yellow cast of the flame, inseparable from the use of petroleum, a piece of camphor can be placed in the reservoir, such piece to be replaced when it has disappeared. This will slightly improve matters, but, of course, the light will still be of a yellow tinge, and the faint blue glasses or modifiers are desirable for proper effect.

CHAPTER X.

DARK GROUND ILLUMINATION

Dark ground illumination.—I have come across a great many microscopists who have never seen the beautiful effects which can be obtained by this method, and more who were in difficulty about being unable to get it always with certainty If the foregoing remarks as to critical illumination have been followed, there will be no difficulty remaining Critical illumination is when the object is at the apex of a solid cone of light, which apex is itself in the focus of the objective Dark ground illumination is when the object is at the apex of a hollow cone of light under similar circumstances The cone of light is made hollow by inserting into a carrier made to receive it a central stop. so proportioned that it blocks out all the direct light the objective lens is capable of receiving The field without the object is dark, but when the object is inserted the oblique rays of the outside of cone, too slanting to reach the lens of themselves, are concentrated on the object and reflected from underside of cover glass on to it till it shines out as though it were self-luminous, the field remaining as a black, or almost black, background. Its best effects are on objects of a certain thickness, it not being so suitable or beautiful for squeezed out flat mounts as for objects mounted without pressure and in their natural form.

Polyzoa, Zoophytes, Foraminifera, water fleas and living animals in water generally are indescribably beautiful examined by this method. If living water creatures are put in a trough with glass cover such as is sold for the purpose, they can be seen in their natural living condition with the internal organs of the transparent kinds open to inspection and all their anatomy displayed at once Any insect mounted in fluid is a suitable object and, in fact, few objects are unsuitable providing they do not require very high powers to see them at all or are smashed so flat that they cannot be lighted up   Mr Julius Rheinberg, F.R M.S., designed a method of double colour illumination based on this method which is always popular and admired. Instead of a black ground he has a coloured one, a central stop of the desired colour being placed where the black opaque one is generally put This gives a coloured field of view and objects can be seen with white light on a coloured field; or by placing a central stop of one colour with a ring margin of another colour, which colours the outer portion of the hollow cone of light. the contrasting colours do not mix but the field remains the colour of the central stop and the object appears the colour of the external ring. The colours must be suitably contrasted, the central stop always being the darker or denser, but the effect to the eye is beautiful if object and colour be suited to each other. These coloured stops and rings can be obtained in stained gelatine, already prepared, from any optician very cheaply, and should be in every outfit where a condenser exists. The black stops can be procurable in wheel form in a series or can be cut out of thin black card. Several of these. different in size, will be required, as if too large they obstruct too much light and the effect is not brilliant, whilst if too small, the field does not remain dark For an inch lens a stop of about $\frac{3}{4}$ inch diameter will do as a first experiment, but the size depends on the aperture of lens and must be proportioned to it. If a few discs of thin glass be obtained to fit the carrier under the condenser various sizes can be tried by punching out stops from black paper and gumming them on. After the size from the lens in use has been found, a metal stop can be made of the size, if the whole series as sold by the opticians be not purchased.

There is an adjustable central stop now to be had, the invention of Mr. W. R. Traviss. This is capable of enlargement or diminution on the principle of a reversed iris diaphragm. It enables the exact size of stop to be obtained at once, being adjustable in place. It is, however, very delicate and must be treated as gently as the escapement of a watch, but properly and carefully used, it is a most useful piece of apparatus, as the blackest field and brightest image is available

Fig. 38.—Stop Closed.   Fig. 38a—Stop Fully Open.

without loss of time in trying which stop is the most desirable.

It is by no means impossible to get something akin to the above effects without a condenser. It will not be as good and will take more time to arrange, but the absence of condenser or spot lens does not imply you cannot get some form of dark ground illumination. If some spots of black paper are cut, say, one-third the

diameter of the bull's-eye, and are stuck on its centre
on the flat side, it can be placed under the stage and
at a distance below to be ascertained only by experiment. It should be arranged with the flat side up
and with the optic axis passing through its centre.
Some position will readily be found where any object
on the stage appears light on a dark ground when
observed through the tube. The gelatine in which
sweets are wrapped can be used on the bull's-eye to
get Mr. Rheinberg's multicolour effects. After the
position for bull's-eye has been found at which the
best effect is secured, care must be taken that neither
microscope nor bull's-eye is shifted in changing slides,
but the extra trouble to get this effect is well worth
taking, as once seen, it will not be long before an
efficient condenser will be coveted, and then a microscopist is born.

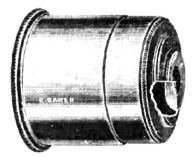

Fig. 39.—Spot Lens for Low Powers.

The paraboloid.—This is an appendage to the
microscope once very much used to get dark ground
illumination. It is a solid piece of glass, plane at
bottom and hollow semi-spherical at top and formed
into a parabola on its sides. It is achromatic because
it reflects only without refraction. The rays entering
at bottom pass upwards without deviation until they
impinge upon the internal surface of the paraboloid,
where they are totally reflected to its focus, which is

in the centre of the hollow spherical curved recess at top. (See Fig. 40.) If the bottom of the plane surface be blocked out with a patch stop the right size to cover the field of the objective lens, such field will be black and not illuminated with direct light. Then, if an object be placed on the stage in the focus of the parabola, it will be lit up by the rays of light which pass outside the central stop, and the object will appear bright on a black ground, as though it were self-luminous. This, with many other pieces of apparatus found in microscopes of a few years back, is practically

Fig. 40. Paraboloid.

superseded by the substage condenser, which will do everything that can be done in this direction, as well as some other things that the paraboloid cannot do. It cannot give very oblique rays, so is not suited to any objective except of narrow angle, whilst the substage condenser of wide angle can always be used at narrower angles than its maximum.

There has been, recently, a somewhat novel modification of the parabola introduced, which requires oiling to the slip to make continuous optical contact and which is of such wide angle that it will do more than the substage condenser. It will shew living bacteria under the highest powers, bright on a dark ground, but its use is not very general. Dark ground work, whilst pleasurable, has not the highest scientific value, measurements of objects thus displayed being unreliable, although the pictures shewn are far the more beautiful.

The action of this accessory depending upon the property of the parabola to reflect parallel rays to a definite point, it is essential that the plane mirror be used with it and that the bull's-eye be correctly disposed to render the light incident on the mirror truly parallel

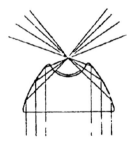

Fig 41.—Course of Rays in Paraboloid

New dark ground condenser with spherical reflecting surfaces —This dark ground condenser was designed, and is primarily intended for, the examination, under high powers, of living unstained bacteria. As it brings the rays to a focus by reflection only and not by refraction it is absolutely free from chromatic aberration and, owing to the design and disposition of the two reflecting surfaces, the various forms of spherical aberration are reduced to a minimum. They are present in a far less degree than in the most carefully ground paraboloid, which surface it is mechanically impossible to polish absolutely true to figure. There is a central stop shewn in figure to prevent passage of the central rays, and the peripheral rays meeting the surface inside the glass, are reflected within it to the side of lower glass whence they are again reflected at an oblique angle to the object. The top of this condenser has to make optical contact with underside of slide by the interposition of a drop of immersion oil. This makes optical continuity and avoids reflection either from top surface of condenser or underside of slide. It does not appear to be generally known that ordinary dark ground illumination for low powers with

Fig. 42.—Oil Immersion Reflecting Condenser.

the Abbe condenser used completely is much improved by filling the gap between top of condenser and the slide with oil or even glycerine. It entirely obviates loss of rays by reflection and greatly enhances the illumination. It would, of course, be troublesome to clean off oil if a number of slides were being rapidly shewn, but if the slide is to remain for any time under observation, the improvement is worth the trouble.

As it is considered by the most eminent expert desirable that the effective aperture of the condenser for dark ground illumination should be three times as great as the effective aperture of the objective lens, the power of thus increasing the effective aperture should not be neglected. Cedar-wood oil, which is the immersion oil to use, must be cleaned off with benzole or xylol, but for ordinary everyday use, glycerine will serve as a substitute. It is easily cleaned off with a moistened linen rag from both slide and lens top and the slight loss, owing to its lower index of refraction for this particular purpose with an Abbe condenser, can be disregarded. The general improvement of using some immersion fluid can hardly be contested.

With powers lower than one inch it will be sometimes difficult to get dark ground with the top of condenser in place. To remedy this, the top is made detachable and the lower power under-glass alone left in use   It will then be found that the condenser, or remaining part of it, must be lowered to get the best effect.

There are many expensive and complicated accessories adapted to various special uses, but as this is essentially a book for beginners, and as the use of these accessories needs special training and knowledge, they are not treated of here   Any optician's list will illustrate them and the more advanced works will explain them, but the more general and everyday apparatus has been described so that any person possessing an ordinary type of instrument may be shewn its uses and pleasures   The present aim is not to instruct the advanced student, but to show the beginner how to get enjoyment and recreation from a moderately priced and not too elaborate an instrument

CHAPTER XI

CARE OF THE MICROSCOPE.

Care of the microscope —A microscope is a delight to the user, and is worth caring for. It should always be put away out of the reach of dust and dirt, and if it requires taking to pieces to put away in its wooden case, it is better to make an ornament of it, always on view, and purchase a glass shade to cover it If these are made of thin glass they are too fragile, but there is a kind made of a heavy type which are to be seen in every up-to-date dairyman's window full of eggs. These are quite a trade thing, and your dairy shop-keeper wherever you are will, no doubt, tell you where to get them These also make good, strong and cheap home aquaria if bought small.

If the slides of the microscope have any shake, the adjusting screws must be gently turned to close it up If they work stiffly they should be slackened, but before doing this try a little vaseline on the edges, as the stiffness may be caused by a gummy grease having become stuck to dust. If the rack is too stiff try cleaning it out with the end of a wooden match, and putting on a very little vaseline by the same means. All water should be carefully removed from the stage or any portion of the instrument as soon as spilled. If immersion oil should ever be used, the lenses must be wiped with benzole on a soft cloth before putting them away; not washed with it, but let the cloth be just damped with the benzole. Oil on slides should also be removed before putting them in their box As the beautiful finish on the microscope is lacquer put on a high polish, no alcohol or methylated spirit may be used on any part of it as this will dissolve the lacquer off. All lenses not in use should be put away out of reach of dust If eye pieces or draw tube stick too tightly a wipe with a cloth moistened with benzole will remove the grease and dirt, and a trifling amount of vaseline rubbed on with the finger and wiped off again will make them go easily into their place.

The little clips on the stage will sometimes get bent upwards, so that they do not grip They can be taken out and gently bent a little downwards at point and replaced, but do not make them grip too tightly, as it should be possible to move the slide about under them quite easily.

If the mirror will not stay at the correct angle after placing it there, it must be sprung out of the letter C ring, and the ring slightly closed together at its points, and the frame sprung in again, noting that the small indentations in the frame engage the projecting points on the ring. Should it be a screw adjuster the remedy is obvious

Above all, be careful in altering anything The microscope is a delicate instrument and needs gently using. It is not a steam engine, and is not able to bear rough handling. If it needs any of the little things done that have been mentioned, think why and wherefore before adjusting, and if you are not mechanically inclined get a skilled friend to do it for you. If in a big town, take it to an optician, who will do any slight adjustments really required at a reasonable price It is new or damaged parts that cost the money.

Care for it well, keep it clean, treat it gently, and it will last for ever.

CHAPTER XII

EXAMINING UNMOUNTED OBJECTS.

Examining unmounted objects. — It sometimes happens that a microscope is bought with just a few slides, and when these have been regarded over and over again a few times, and the expense of purchasing a new supply has been considered, the instrument is put away, and the first glow of interest dies down entirely. This need not be, even if no slides are at hand of mounted specimens A great deal of interesting work can be done on unmounted objects. There is all around us quite an inexhaustible variety of material from which one can get both amusement and instruction. If low powers be used a far better idea can frequently be formed of many subjects in their natural and unprepared condition. It is only the best way of looking at any kind of object which must be sought for.

Amongst opaque objects, lighted with bull's-eye from the top, or with the side reflector, can be named fungi, mosses, green mould on bark of trees, fences or walls, mildew from boots out of use, seeds, spore from underside of fern leaves, leaves, pollen from flowers, petals of flowers, eggs of insects, especially butterflies' eggs found on leaves, nettle stings. cheese mites, butterflies' wings, bugs, fleas, bees, flies, maggots, caterpillars, the green fly or Aphis found on plants in rapidly increasing colonies, in fact, insects generally, spiders, etc. It is only necessary to devise some temporary means of attachment to hold the object still on a piece of card The writer has frequently .put an insect on to a piece of sticky fly-paper,

F

placed as a small patch on a piece of cardboard, in order to study its form and action alive. The above list could, with a little thought, be extended almost indefinitely.

For objects of a transparent kind to be examined by transmitted light, a plain glass slip is placed upon the stage, the subject placed on it, and if well displayed no more need be done; but, generally, a drop of water added and a small cover glass put on top enables much more to be made out. There are troughs made to hold water in which living objects taken from water can be examined Small slips, 3×1 inches, are also made with a concavity ground in one side, which are sufficiently large to hold water life, and if these be used with a glass cover over the water, little more is needed if the object is not to be preserved A drop of water small enough can usually be put on the object by means of a fountain pen filler, sold at a penny Amongst this class of object may be enumerated, water life of microscopical character in rain gutters, stagnant pools, larvæ of various flies which are aquatic in their early stages, young tadpoles, etc. Under skin, peeled off leaves, fibres of vegetable substances, teased out to separate pollen grains, very thin sections cut from young plant stems, with a sharp razor both across and longways from the stem. Pollen grains can be made especially interesting, as, if wetted and a cover glass applied, the growth of tubercules can be seen gradually elongating from some portion of the grain which eventually discharge the fovilla or content like a cloud of smoke. This is how the pollen grain under natural conditions fecundates the other portion of the flower and leads to the development of seed Flies' wings are good objects as temporary transparencies So also are fibres of cotton, wool, hemp, silk, etc., when teased out with a needle to display individual fibres The difference between these various fibres once learnt can be very useful as well as amusing. Even a smear of jam or marmalade will, if a cover glass be laid over it, reveal the structure of the vegetable substance composing it. The circulation of sap in the leaves of small water plants or the circulation of blood in a tadpole's tail can all be displayed in this way.

A very little thought will suggest further examples, so there is plenty of material without one resorting to mounted preparations

If the instrument be fitted with a polariscope accessory, there are fine effects to be got with very thin shavings of various woods. These had better be placed on a small patch on the plain glass slip with a drop of turps on them, and then the thin cover glass applied, as they are more transparent under this treatment. Corn parings from your poor toes, scrapings from the human nail, scrapings of whalebone, different kinds of thin papers, cotton threads, tiny pieces of fine muslin, a pinch of silver sand, or any other sand, hairs of all kinds, etc , if treated as above, make good temporary polariscopic display subjects. The finest and best easily made show objects for this accessory are crystals of salts A solution in the bottom of an egg-cup can be made and one drop placed on a clean glass slip, which can be dried and examined, or if the slip be warm and the solution strong, can be examined whilst it is drying, and the process of crystallisation watched. These slides, if kept clean, can be used again and again, and are the easiest method of multiplying a lot of interesting objects, as the number of salts is indefinitely large. For a beginning, try copper sulphate, chloride of ammonia (sal ammoniac), a drop out of the battery will do, sulphate of soda, alum, borax, common soda, oxalic acid, saltpetre, etc , in fact, all salts and their crystallisation can be regarded as supplying good objects for the microscope If sap from a plant be squeezed out in a drop on to a glass slip, some crystallisable salt is sure to be present.

Starch grains from various cereals, obtained by grating and washing and then allowed to settle, are polariscopic objects, as are also grit from new sponges, and scales of all fishes. All these can hardly, as temporary mounts, compare with the specially prepared purchased specimens, but are well worthy of examination, and provide a never ending choice of new subjects.

A living water flea from a pond, if put in a sunk cell with a little water and covered with a cover glass, makes a delightful display, as, owing to its transparency, the whole interior anatomy is displayed.

If one has a spot lens or condenser to get dark ground effects, all the water denizens can be regarded in their natural conditions, light on a dark ground. A prolonged examination of their habits and life is possible, as many will live and thrive for a long time in the glass trough. If a decoction of hay be made as

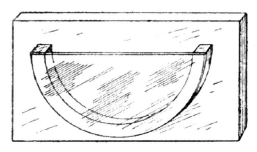

Fig. 43.—Glass Trough for Examining Living Objects in Water

one makes tea, and then strained and put outdoors, in a few days it will be found teeming with minute forms of life, generated from germs floating in the air, which develop if dropped into a nourishing medium. With the aid of the spot lens these can be seen flitting about with great rapidity. They are transparent to the great flood of light, which obscures them if transmitted light be used, but as white on black the living creatures can be easily seen; but the delicate details of the finer structure of the smaller specimens of this type hardly belongs to the early stages of the beginner

Try various subjects in various ways, and the best method of making the most of an object unmounted will soon be acquired.

The object of a mounted preparation is rather preservation than ease of seeing. Of course, there is much that cannot be seen, especially of internal structures, until the object has been treated in various ways, suited to bring into prominence what we wish to see, or to dissolve out that which obscures After one has got used to the temporary method, the desire to preserve permanently some specially interesting object will be aroused. It will then not be long before dexterity acquired in handling the tiny specimens, added to a little knowledge and a lot of practice, will develop the diffident beginner into an expert mounter One's own mounting is generally valued the most, and one learns structure whilst manipulating them.

The microscope on seaside holidays —When one is away at the seaside, many an hour can be spent in looking for objects that cannot be found at home A walk without an object, even in a salubrious atmosphere, has not the same interest as a tramp around with some definite purpose in view, and the seaside walks, during one's holiday, can be combined with the acquisition of sufficient material to last a long time It may even add to one's collection of objects something of permanent value and, in any case, will enlarge the individual perception of the marvellous world we inhabit Further, if a small collection be obtained the first day or so, the misery of a wet day at the seaside will cease to exist, as the detailed examination of fresh wonders will prevent moping about waiting for the weather to clear To take the microscope, unless it be a very heavy one, will not greatly increase the baggage, and that with a trough and a few bottles to carry in the pocket is all that will be required. After a very little practice in microscope using, it will be found very pleasurable to look through the finds of the day, which, even if not rare, will be quite of a new type

Foraminifera, or small shells of single celled animals, will often be found in the little ripples of sand left by the receding tide These are sometimes of great variety, but all are worthy of regard.

Seaweed, or portions of seaweed, will frequently be found to bear living animals, on leaves or stem If so, the portion can be cut away and dropped into one of the bottles previously filled with sea water They will live long enough to expand their tentacles, and make fine objects to view in the trough.

The slimy green on an old sea-wall, or rock can be taken home in the same way, or a piece of the rock broken off with the growth put into a wide mouth bottle.

Prawns, shrimps, and small shore crabs, make a good and interesting study for the hand lens, which should always be carried on these trips

It is quite possible to stock a marine aquarium on a holiday with one's finds. and if arranged with a few pieces of rock and some sea sand at bottom, with enough vegetation of a marine character, suitably disposed to keep the water aerated, it will be found almost as easy to keep a marine aquarium in order as a fresh water one.

The life histories of the smaller denizens of the deep can then be studied at home, and, even if a study be not made of it, there will always be found plenty of entertainment and elevating amusement.

Some of the larger books deal copiously with this side of microscopy, and if the reader be really interested in it. there is ample information with description of method and lists of suitable material to obtain.

The beginner, however, can chance what he gets and saves, but the slight effort, here suggested, is well worth the little trouble it will involve.

The home aquarium.—The budding microscopist who once sees some of the denizens of water taken from a pond will wish he could always have a supply of such interesting objects on hand. This is quite possible, and without expense. All that is required is a fine muslin net, fitted with a glass tube at the

APPARATUS FOR COLLECTING, PREPARING, MOUNTING AND STORING SPECIMENS.

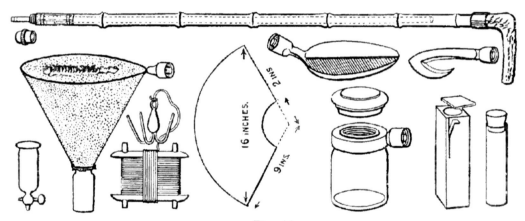

Fig. 44.

Collecting Stick to which Net is attached.
Collecting Net.
Pattern to Cut Muslin for Net.
Spoon to attach to Stick.
Bottle to attach to Stick.
Hook for cutting Weeds.
Drag Hook for searching a Pond.

bottom. The water taken up is strained through the net and the living creatures are concentrated in the glass tube where they are easily seen, and from which they can easily be transferred to other receptacles.

These may be ordinary wide-mouth bottles obtainable in any household, and which will serve as well as those specially sold for the purpose. They need not be too large, as it may be desirable to keep certain captures separate from others, as it will soon be learnt that eat or be eaten is a natural law A very little observation and a few losses of choice captures will soon teach the collector what to keep separate. The apparatus needed can be obtained from the leading opticians, if purse is well filled, but home-made substitutes are just as efficient.

A few sweeps of the net in an accessible pond will bring to light an unsuspected quantity and variety of aquatic life, and if it be examined in the water trough, a new world will be opened out To preserve one's captures, procure a few glass jam jars with small stones and a handful of sand at the bottom. These can be filled with pond water, and the material at bottom is preferably taken from a pond bottom, as it will then contain eggs, larvæ, or embryos of living creatures which will in time develop at home and their life cycle may be profitably watched. It will be necessary to put some weed from the pond into each stock jar, as the action of light on the growing plant develops an aeration of the water, keeps it sweet and healthy, and it will not require to be changed at all if ordinary dirt and dust be excluded by a piece of glass, such as an old negative, placed on top of each jar.

The result of any outing can be added to the jars, the creatures can live their lives under your eyes, and you will always have some living object to shew friends. Most pond weed has at times beautiful forms of life growing on it, and sprigs should be placed in the trough and looked over. It is impossible here to give a list of names, but after all, it is not the name that matters. Knowledge of a subject does not consist in knowing a lot of scientific Latin names of natural history objects, but on the mastery of how the creatures live their little lives, as important to them as ours to us, and this real knowledge can be learnt by observing them. If scientific classification is desired, it can be found in specially written books which treat of it, but knowledge at first hand and by one's own observations has a habit of sticking, whilst names and classification have the tendency to be forgotten except by the expert.

The birth, growth and development of some forms of pond life are extremely interesting. With a water trough to examine and a few jars of material, there will be a perpetual source of amusement and instruction, and the living creatures examined under natural conditions are much more beautiful than the most expensive set of mounted slides, as no mounted slide, however well prepared, can give the motion we call life.

The living creatures in the jars are removed when required by a short length of glass tubing open at each end. If the top be closed by the finger and the bottom forced down into the water and near to anything it is desired to capture, the stopped end can be opened by raising the finger which closes it and the water near the other end will rush into the tube carrying the animal with it. The top can now be closed again and the tube removed from the jar. If its lower end be placed on the top of the trough and the top finger lifted, the water and all that it contains will drop into the trough. These troughs are comparatively cheap and last a long while; they will never wear out if not broken.

Weeds growing far out in the pond can be drawn in with a hook tied on a length of cord, and mud from the bottom can be obtained by tying cord on the neck of a bottle or jar and drawing it along the bottom of a pond after throwing it out some distance and letting

it sink   Water fleas, larvæ of flies and beetles, water
spiders, etc., are easy to find, and if fortunate enough
to find some of the beautiful polyzoa, of which there
are many varieties growing on the weeds, you will
have secured treasure enough to last a long time and
make you want to search for more.

Information as to life histories of aquatic inhabitants
will be found in books and the names and classification given, and the study of one pond may be made a
lifetime's work if done thoroughly and systematically.

CHAPTER XIII.

MOUNTING OBJECTS FOR THE MICROSCOPE.

Mounting objects.—The primary object of mounting is to preserve as well as display. Different subjects require different treatment, and the description of one

MOUNTING TOOLS.

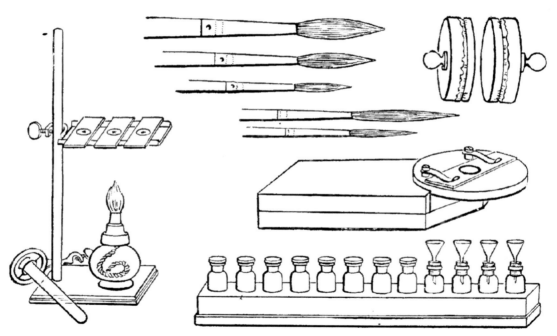

Fig. 45.—Spirit Lamp, Brushes, Cover Glass Cleaners, Turntable, and Stand for Bottles.

method only is not sufficient. Several methods must be given, as that which will display and will preserve one certain object, may be far from the best method of treating another.

The methods, however, resolve themselves into certain classes, and all objects can be referred to one or other of these classes. They are called opaque mounting, fluid mounting, or balsam mounting. The primary consideration of all three methods of treatment is absolute cleanliness, and it will surprise the beginner to find how easy it is to mount what is not required in the way of dirt and undesired substances. On the other hand, he will, at the commencement, at least find it difficult to mount and display the object he desires to fix, and nothing else but the object. A glass may seem clear, fluid and balsam may to ordinary vision seem quite clear, and the air of the room may appear to be all that is desirable, yet, unless training in clean and exact methods have been practised, there will be found, when the object is examined under the magnifying power of a good microscope, lots of undesirable material. Hence, care in cleaning glasses, the filtering of fluids, and the closing of bottles the instant their contents have been withdrawn, are absolutely essential. Cleanliness in all operations, clean and orderly methods of working, and clean places in which to store materials are necessary, so necessary that carelessness and slovenly methods can never produce a good permanent mount. The usage of the present time is to mount all preparations on glass slides. These are of special flatted glass, and of regular size, three inches by one inch, the edges being ground after cutting, so that they can be safely handled without fear of cuts or scratches They are quite cheap, and are sold in various thicknesses and qualities, the cheapest costing 3d. a dozen, so that there is no saving in making them for ourselves. They should be, and usually are, of picked flat glass, and the uniformity of size leads to ease and neatness of storage. Odd sizes and styles are troublesome to use and a nuisance to store, so keep to the stock size.

In all styles of mounting, the object is covered by a very thin kind of glass, which is made in circles, squares, and oblongs of various sizes, as may be suited for the subject in hand The thin glass can be procured for home cutting, but the prepared covers are better, and except for very special purposes the beginner will find the odd sizes quite unnecessary. The cover glasses are made in three thicknesses, the thinner being for the most delicate and fine objects to be examined with high powers. This thickness is called No. 1, No. 3 being the thickest used for fluid mounts and for covering dry cells, No. 2 being intermediate. They are sold by the ounce, the thickest size costing about 3s oz., the No 2, 4s oz , and the very thinnest 5s They are sold in $\frac{1}{4}$ oz. boxes, and as they are thin and light a $\frac{1}{4}$ oz box of No. 3 in assorted sizes for 1s. will meet every requirement of the beginner. It will be as well at first to keep to one size, making the first efforts uniform in appearance, and the size known as $\frac{7}{8}$ No 3 will be sufficient with which to commence These cover glasses are somewhat fragile, and the knack of cleaning them is best acquired in the thicker kind There is, for those who do count the cost, an arrangement on the market for cleansing these cover glasses consisting of two flat covered plates. This is efficient in use and economical of glasses, but a few broken glasses to acquire the delicate manipulative skill required in handling is not a big price to pay, and a delicate sense of touch having once been secured, it will be rare to break one in cleaning A broken glass in cleaning is a sure warning that sufficient care in handling is not being taken, and this warning should be heeded. A broken cover glass is not much, but the same want of care may entirely spoil an object difficult to procure again.

The cover glasses are, as a rule, reasonably clean from obstinate dirt, the dust and foreign surface stains being easily removed by damping the fingers and gently rubbing the glass between the fingers through a clean linen handkerchief. The slides, however, are usually more dirty, and sometimes greasy, and it is as well to give them a good clean when first bought. Soda in water is as good as anything, and a final clean, just before use, with a clean linen handkerchief just moistened, not wetted, with methylated spirits. There is also another kind of slide, useful at times, which has

MOUNTING TOOLS.

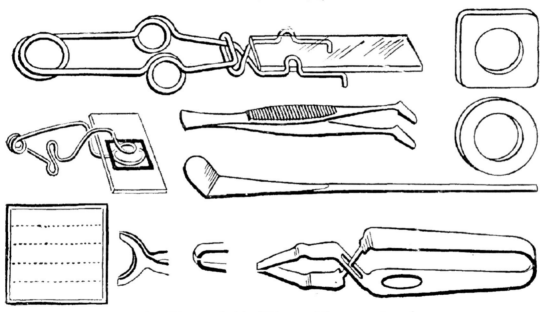

Fig. 46.—Clips to hold Slides whilst warming them. Rims for Cells, Tweezers, Labels, and Flat Lifter to take delicate objects out of Solution.

been hollowed out by grinding and the surface polished. These are known as sunk cells. These have a shallow depression, capable of holding the prepared object if thin. These recessed glasses are also useful in order to examine small unmounted objects in water, such as water-fleas, etc., as the hollow space serves to confine the object in the field of view. If the object be too thick to go into a small cell, a rim ot some material must be put on to the slide to raise the glass cover, and leave room for the object without subjecting it to pressure. Such rims make the slide into what is called a cell, and anything which cannot stand pressure must be mounted in some kind of cell. The rims are attached to the glass with various kinds of cement. For dry-mounted objects, almost any sound form of cement will serve, but for cells to hold fluid the cement must be tenacious rather than brittle, and one is described a little later. The rims are made in tin, aluminium, and vulcanite, each costing 1s. a gross, also in glass, which are more expensive. It will hardly be possible to do much mounting, or to do it well without what is called a turntable. This is a brass disc, spinning on its centre, and usually carrying two clips like those on the stage of the microscope in order to hold the glass in any desired position on the face of the disc. A turntable, to be really useful, should spin freely, yet without side shake, and should go for about half a minute. In use, a slide or slip is centred on the turntable, making sure that middle of slip and centre of turntable coincide. There is usually a ring to take the corners of the slip, which assists this to be done. If the slip be in place and a spin with the left hand be given to disc, and a camel or sable hair brush, charged with paint, be touched on to it, a ring will be described, the size being proportioned to the position of brush away from the centre. There are, usually, one or two gauge rings engraved on the top of turntable, so that it is quite easy to produce a circle in varnish, paint, or cement of any size. The same little tool is used to finish the edges of all cover glasses where the ring of varnish is a protection and a desirable finish to any slide. Beside the articles mentioned, there will be required two or three small brushes. Camel hair at 1d. each have been recommended, but

the writer prefers sables, costing a little more, as
these are much better for the purpose. A few needles
of various sizes driven into penholders will be wanted
to lower cover glasses into place and adjust objects on
the slide to arrange them in their best position. If
dissecting is done, one or two scalpels and a fine pair
of scissors will be requisite, but these can all be got
as necessity arises, and the cost is but small.

For opaque mounting, which is recommended as a
commencement, the above-mentioned articles with a
bottle of cement and a bottle of finishing varnish will
be required

For balsam mounting, which is embedding the
object in a preservative medium of about the same
density as glass, there will be wanted, in addition to
the articles required for opaque or dry mounting, a
bottle of balsam in benzole or xylol, which is easier
to use than pure balsam. pure alcohol, clove oil, turps,
and a bottle of ten per cent. caustic soda.

In balsam mounting the object is generally squeezed
flat and sections of tissue, both animal and vegetable,
are also thus mounted

It may be of interest to note that opticians keep
small boxes of insect and other preparations already
dissected and ready for mounting, and the first
attempts can well be made with these. They are, if
intended to be mounted in balsam, all ready for use,
and only need a preliminary soaking in turpentine to
expel the air. It is very essential that all air be removed, or the finished slide will be full of bubbles
and therefore spoiled as an object of interest. The
boxes of objects are all named and classed, and each
contains a slip stating the best method of mounting
to exhibit them properly, and are sold in considerable
variety. A little practice will soon give confidence,
and one will soon learn what to do and what to avoid

It is well to take difficulties one at a time and the

prepared objects will leave a beginner little to do or think about at the time of mounting except the clean, neat, and orderly methods of manipulation which are necessary.

Dry mounting.—To proceed with dry mounting, the object, whether leaf, butterfly's wing or part of it, leg of insect, seeds, or pollen, must be perfectly dry.

Take a glass slide and gum a circle of dull black paper in the centre. This dull paper can be bought at opticians, already gummed on back. If the object is thin, run a ring of gold size on the slide with the aid of a turntable; or, if the object is thick, affix a tin or vulcanite ring. Put a small spot of gum in the centre of ring on the black paper and allow it to dry. Gum tragacanth is better than ordinary gum, as the former does not dry glossy.

When ready to mount the object, breathe on the gum surface of black paper and the gum will get tacky. Then place the object in the exact position and touch it down to the tacky gum with a needle. Leave an hour or two for all moisture to dry out, and attach the cover glass. This is best affected by putting the slide on the turntable and giving the top edge of cell a thin coating of gold size or the cement described later. In a short time the cement will be tacky, and the cover glass rested on one edge of the cell by holding between the thumb and finger of left hand and dropped on to a needle held in the right hand and gently lowered into place. It can be adjusted perfectly central with the needle and then pressed down on the gold size or cement. The next day it can be again put on the turntable and a ring of black varnish neatly laid around its edge finishes the slide. If the cell and object be perfectly dry, it will be permanent. If any moisture be left in the cell, there will at times be found fungoid growths or cloudiness. A label should be attached shewing the class, name, and any necessary

G

particulars about the object, so that it can be identified without putting it under the microscope. Suitable labels, ready gummed, are sold for sixpence a gross. There are various kinds of finishing varnishes to be obtained and in any colour. Black is the most usual, but whatever be selected keep to the same one, as a collection of slides looks much more presentable when similarity of finish and labelling give a uniform appearance to them. For a black varnish, the writer has not come across anything better than gold size with sufficient printer's black ink to make it sufficiently dense. The spirit varnishes dry quicker and are somewhat easier to apply, but they are very brittle and chip with the slightest jar or rubbing, whilst the blackened gold size is tough. Printer's ink is only used because it is the finest lampblack in oil varnish obtainable, and, being already ground, there are not likely to be the granular unmixed particles which detract from the finish when the lampblack is home ground. If too thick, a little naphtha or benzole can be used to get it to a workable consistency, as these dry out quicker than turpentine.

For balsam mounting, the object must be embedded in Canada balsam, which is a pure form of turpentine. This is best used as prepared by the dealers diluted with xylol, or benzole, used to thin it out, as this enables air bubbles to escape, and air bubbles are the bugbear of balsam mounting. The objects need entirely dehydrating, that is, every atom of water must be removed as there is no sympathy or tendency to amalgamate between balsam and water. The slightest dampness leads to cloudy mounts, and a damp object placed in balsam cannot be dehydrated easily. If the object be an insect, or part of one, it must be cleaned and softened by placing for a time in a solution of caustic potash, which should be made of one ounce of caustic potash to one quart of water. This may mean

for an hour or two or may mean for several days,
according to its hardness at first. Let us suppose an
insect such as a metropolitan B-flat. It should be
placed in a little of the caustic potash solution and
covered from dust. The next day try if it be soft by
touching it with a thin strip of wood, such as a piece
off an ordinary matchbox, which is sufficiently flexible
if the flat of the wood be pressed on the insect. If
soft and anything of its internal anatomy tends to
exude, soak it in plain water till the potash be removed; two or three changes in a saucer will do. Then
with a cheap camel hair brush endeavour to press out
the body contents. Do *not* put a brush into the caustic
to do this or it will be spoiled, wash the object in water
first. If the animal will not go clear and reasonably
transparent, return it to the potash for further softening. When the contents of the body are rolled out,
and this must be done gently so that the internals are
given up without breaking the external integument, it
can be arranged with your brush in clean water on a
glass slip. If the softening has been correctly timed,
the limbs can be arranged symmetrically around it and
its mouth parts spread out to display the suctorial
organs. Another slip can now be placed upon it and
tied with thread to keep it flat whilst the water is
drained off. It must then be placed as it is, between
the glasses, into alcohol, and for an object of this kind
methylated spirit will serve for the first bath. Alcohol
has a great affinity for water and will abstract water
from anything placed in it; and the object will be full
of alcohol instead of water. There will still, however,
be a little water left in the object because the alcohol
has become diluted in its turn, and the operation must
be repeated with pure spirit. These solutions can be
returned to a stock-bottle for further use as a first bath,
so the spirit is not all wasted and can be used again and
again for the earlier dips. Finally, the object should

be placed in a bath of pure spirit and the thread cut. It will now be possible to slide the creature off quite stiff and flat into a tiny saucer of clove oil, which removes the alcohol while allowing no air to enter As soon as it sinks to the bottom of the little saucer it can be taken out and dropped into turpentine, where it can remain until one is ready to mount it. When ready, it can be taken out and laid on the centre of a glass slip and arranged just how it is desired to be Then drain off the turpentine and Canada balsam in xylol should be dropped on it A fountain pen filler is a good instrument to use to take the balsam from the bottle and place it on the slide, as the rubber teat at the end gives perfect control of the quantity, which should be just enough to cover the animal and no more. If an excess be used it will ooze out all over the slip and need a lot of cleaning off A neat mounter soon learns to judge the quantity required so that no trimming is necessary If too little is used it can be added by means of the pen-filler after glass is put on. The glass cover can now be taken by the edges between finger and thumb of left hand, of course after it is perfectly cleaned, and with the third finger behind it, rest one edge on the slip. Have one of the handled needles in the right hand and rest the top edge of cover glass on the needle If the needle be gently and very slowly lowered, the glass will rest on it and it can be allowed to go right down The balsam, meanwhile, having touched the lower edge of cover will gradually creep right across it as it descends, leaving no room for air bubbles to form at all. If the operation is hurried, or if the glass be dropped, it is certain the balsam will not have time to displace the air, but will entangle a host of bubbles, which will necessitate beginning all over again If there be but one bubble, tilting the slide may cause it to rise to the highest side, especially if it be placed in a warm place whilst a trifle tilted. Should too little balsam be used so that the cover glass is not filled underneath with the balsam, take the pen-filler with a little balsam in the tube. and gently put a spot on the edge of the cover where the balsam *does* reach the edge and it will run under and fill up the vacant space, but do not attempt to add the balsam to the vacant part or you will entangle an air bubble with it.

The slide can now be put away in a warm place for a few days, when the balsam will be found hardened Any rough edges or blobs can be scraped away gently till slide is clean, finally cleaning off with a rag moistened with methylated spirit If balsam is not very hard this must be done with great care not to displace the mounting

A balsam mount does not really require a varnished or cemented ring, but it is a protection against displacement as well as a finish to ring it Place the slide on the turntable, and give the turntable a spin It will probably be out of centre, and must be adjusted till the edge of cover glass seems to remain still when the turntable is revolved. When centred a very fine line can be placed around the edge, and a very thin coat must be given. Otherwise, whatever is used will creep in underneath the cover, and by mixing with the balsam will ruin your slide. Hollis' glue, which is something like shellac in naphtha, does very well for the first fine ring, but sealing wax in methylated spirit will do as well. The object is only to prevent the finishing varnish entering the mount by mixing with the balsam Either of the above things will be dry in ten minutes if only the thin ledge of the cover glass be filled up If more is put on it will take longer It can now be finally ringed with the gold size and printer's ink. or other selected finish varnish; then when dry labelled and stored

Any insect preparation can be done in the same way

as our B-flat is   Larger insects or harder ones want
more soaking in the potash solution, or if dark in
colour they will need bleaching   If it be desired to
make an object more transparent than the potash will
readily do, it can be cleaned after the potash, soaked
in water and placed for a short time in a bath of a
few crystals of chlorate of potash, to which has been
added 2 to 3 drops of hydrochloric acid   After bleaching, the object must be thoroughly washed and the
methylated spirit treatment proceeded with as before.
Thin sections of plant stems for balsam mounting only
require dehydrating with spirit, etc., as stated above,
unless they are to be stained, which much enhances
their appearance, and differentiates their structure.
Instructions for injecting and staining, however, must
be looked for in more advanced works than this   When
this is to be attempted one is not quite a beginner

If the purchased objects, ready prepared for mounting in balsam, are obtained, they will need a very much
longer soaking in turpentine than those that have re-
mained in some kind of fluid during the whole process,
as the drying out of the water   without substituting
alcohol allows air to thoroughly permeate the dried
object, and it must by prolonged soaking be entirely
displaced by turpentine   Unless this is done, air
bubbles will remain in the finished mount, and it will
be practically impossible to remove them   There are
some rough objects which, after washing, may be dried
between the leaves of a book, but small insects lose
their limbs by the process.   The finished slide always
looks cleaner if the object is dried by alcohol, and if
air never enters during the drying process it does not
need to be removed.   When any object after drying is
not perfectly flat, and its tendency to lift the cover is
so pronounced as to make it impossible to leave the
balsam to harden without the cover lifting, it can be
put away under a tiny weight   such as a small leaden

bullet, which will probably be sufficient to keep the object flat till the balsam is set hard There are also spring clips sold by the opticians for the same purpose, and either is effective. There are many unprepared objects which, like the prepared ones, need no other treatment than soaking for a time in turpentine to displace contained air. The balsam readily mixes with and follows the turpentine. Amongst them are small insects, such as fleas, parasites, and book mites; wings of flies and other insects; wood shavings Sponge spicules can be obtained by washing a new sponge and drying the grit at bottom of jar in which it has been soaked and squeezed. These spicules are parts of the siliceous skeleton of the sponge, and many of the forms are of singular beauty. Feathers or parts of feathers, of birds; hairs of various kinds; silk fibres, teased out with needles to a fluff; cotton fibres, linen and flax fibres; wool; jute; hemp, etc. Learn by observation to discriminate wool from jute, cotton from silk, cotton from wool, and linen from cotton, and be independent of what you may be assured by others as to what things are made of. This is quite easy if a selection of slides be made from things close at hand and labelled, keeping the certainly known substances as standards. Notice the difference between hair from the human head, hairs from dog, cat, rabbit, and mouse. There is an enormous variety of objects in every house Then for crystals. After making them for temporary examination, as previously mentioned, if a peculiarly good specimen is obtained, put a drop of balsam on it when dry and affix a cover glass, and you will in most cases have a permanent mount The few which fail, you will find, is because Canada balsam has a solvent action upon some salts. This power to dissolve crystals, however. is not great, and ceases when the balsam is saturated, so it is only necessary to have a thicker coating to ensure success Crystals that dis-

solve in Canada balsam can be mounted by putting a
drop of castor oil on them instead of balsam, and then
ringing the cover glass with shellac solution instead of
gold size   Castor oil has no action on the salts soluble,
or partially soluble, in balsam, but it is much more
tricky to use, as if the slightest portion oozes out at the
edge it will be almost impossible to seal it down permanently.   It should, therefore, not be attempted till
skill has been acquired.   Almost every known salt
makes a good slide, and some with the polariscope are
simply gorgeous   A whole collection of these can be
made without great expense, and many are at hand in
every home

Then there are the fibres of fruits, jams, etc. These
can be mounted with a cover glass over just as they
are, by putting a smear of them on a slide and fixing
a cover glass.   Most of the commercial varieties need
no preservative   Quite a small quantity will suffice,
but, of course, this is not balsam mounting.   They will
only need ringing when edge is clean   Sections of
stems of plants, or sections of leaves, or the under skin
torn from the leaves of various plants, petals of flowers,
etc , if placed between the two glasses and dehydrated,
soaked in turps and mounted, are of great interest,
and no two are alike   The sections can be cut from
the stem with a sharp razor under water in a bowl,
many in succession being cut from the same piece of
stem, and the thinnest and most transparent selected
for mounting.   They are no good unless at least as
thin or thinner than this piece of paper, but if many
are cut, the spoiled or incomplete ones can be rejected
and the most perfect thin one selected for further
treatment   The cellular structure of plant stems will
surprise one by its complexity the first time it is seen
There are section cutters to be had with screw feed to
give any pre-determined thickness, but the attempt to
do without the mechanical aid is a training for the

hand in itself, and it is good to train the hand as well
as the eye. The scales of various fishes all make good
slides, and are mostly polariscopic, showing brilliant
coloured undulations when the polariser is rotated.
These can be easily mounted by cleaning with brushes
to get off the slime drying quite flat, soaking in turpentine, and mounting in balsam. The eel, plaice, and
sole are usually at hand, and each of them are worth
a lot of trouble to get clean and clear, the eel being
especially good. The claw of spider, foot of fly,
mandibles of spider, parts which can all be got out
without skilled dissection, are easily mounted in balsam by the process first described, and are most interesting. It is impossible to do more than suggest the
kind of thing to practise on, as the number of possible
slides from material near hand is so great that this
book could not pretend to mention all. It is as well
to mount some objects dry, and some in balsam to
compare, as a little information as to form and uses
may be gleaned from each method, and a better understanding of the nature of the object attained

Fluid mounting of objects —This style of mounting
is one which is growing much more popular than it
used to be, and the term fluid mounting is applied to
all those objects which are got up in a medium containing water, whether it be actually fluid or gelatinous
or syrupy. There are various fluids used, according to
the needs of the case, and that which is most suited to
the object in one case, may not be most suited in
another. There is distilled water, camphorated water,
dilute solutions of various neutral salts, carbolic water,
dilute formalin, glycerine, glycerine jelly and various
thick gums containing some preservative. The ideal
universal mountant has yet to be found, and there is
still room for experiment. Glycerine is really good, but
more difficult for the beginner to use than a solution
which dries out at the edge of the cover glass, because

if any glycerine oozes out at the edge of the cover glass
the ordinary cements for sealing do not stick   The
jellies are the easiest perhaps to use, but they have a
nasty knack of shrinking up and leaving air spaces.
On the whole, the writer would recommend for all-
round use at first the adoption of a two per cent solution of formalin.   This was first adopted by Mr C F,
Rousselet, Vice-President of the Royal Microscopical
Society. for mounting his beautiful aquatic preparations extended as in life and with a natural appearance.
All that is lacking is the motion   This is the chief
recommendation of mounting in fluids   There is no
squashing the specimen out of all shape or removing
its internals, but it is mounted in a cell without pressure and its natural appearance is preserved.   An object can be quite quickly mounted if not too delicate,
and the real natural form preserved, bar damage, for
all time.   The formalin is sold by chemists or opticians
who deal in microscopes, in a 40 per cent solution, and
one part of formalin as sold to fifteen parts of distilled
water will be of the right strength   It is a good preservative and can be used in place of spirit to keep
any captured objects till the time arrives when they
can be mounted.   It has a slight, but only slight,
hardening effect, but by no means renders the tissues
stiff and unmanageable as does alcohol   If tap water
containing lime should get into it. there is at times a
tendency for the fluid to go milky or cloudy, but the
re-mounting in this case is so easily accomplished that
it can be universally used till experience justifies the
trial of other methods   Formalin solution is easy to
seal down. its density, the same as water, suits aquatic
organisms better than glycerine and makes the avoid-
ance of air bells easy, as they rise to the surface and
can be pricked off with the point of a dry needle   To
make the solution it is well to boil the distilled water
when procured by standing the bottle containing it in a

saucepan of water and bringing the outer water to the boil. This drives off the contained air and, when cool, the bottle of distilled water can be kept for use It must not be shaken, and in pouring out it should be poured out gently down the side of the bottle into which it is to be transferred so as to avoid the entanglement of air or formation of bubbles The tormalin must be added in its proper proportion by letting it run down the side and not drop into the centre, which might make air bells in the solution. Every object to be mounted in fluid, unless it is a temporary mount, must soak for some days at least in the same kind of solution in which it is to be mounted in order that the fluid may penetrate and fill every portion of it, and in order that any chemical action which might give off a gas in reacting object against fluid, may be fully spent. By this means all after-development of bubbles in the mount may be avoided, and if the fluid be prepared with care and the object well soaked, there will be nothing to spoil a mount but imperfect sealing of the edges With this kind of mounting there is either a sunk cell with a concavity ground in, or a built up cell with a tin, glass, or vulcanite ring. Sometimes if the object be very thin indeed, a ring of varnish of some kind put on the slide by the turntable and a brush will be enough, but the depth of a cell must at least equal the thickness of the object, as otherwise there would be pressure and distortion, and the chief beauty of the whole process " as in life " would be lost Cells are made in various depths and the rings can be got in any thickness and any size They must be stuck on to the glass slide so tightly that there will be no fear of a little variation of temperature by acting differently on the glass and the fluid tending to force them off, or drawing in outside air

A cement for affixing rims to make cells when fluid is to be the mounting medium requires to be suffi-

ciently hard to be adhesive, rigid enough to bear handling, yet elastic enough to stand the trifling differences
of volume due to temperature variation. Glass and the
fluid held in it do not expand or contract in exactly
the same ratio when subjected to changes of temperature, and the cement must break and let in air eventually if not in some slight degree elastic Such a suitable cement can be made as follows: A penny tube
of cycle rubber solution, which is rubber in naphtha, is
emptied into a four ounce bottle, and double its volume
of old thick gold size added, shaking till thoroughly
mixed This must now be placed in a warm place, not
over 150 deg F., in order to drive off the naphtha and
any volatile constituent of the gold size. Whilst this
is being done prepare a thick solution of shellac in
alcohol When the gold size solution does not smell
of naphtha add about twice its volume of shellac solution as thick as can be poured. Thick as old treacle
Stir whilst warm and filter through fine muslin before
cooling, as it is too thick to strain afterwards It can
be thinned at any time by the addition of two or three
drops of alcohol.

Use the cement as thickly as it can be worked to
flow from the brush and make a heavy ring on the glass
the size of the tin or vulcanite ring to be attached.
This sets in about fifteen minutes and dries reasonably
hard in a day This ensures perfect contact of the
cement with the glass slide and, of course, it is better
to prepare a reasonable quantity of slides at one time
whilst at it To cement the ring, take a scraping of
soap from a piece in use and smear on the turntable in
centre.

If using a metal cell, flatten both sides of the ring
on coarse emery cloth; if of vulcanite, use coarse sand-
paper. One of these can now be pressed on to the
soap and adjusted carefully with sufficient firmness to
hold whilst it is cemented all round on its upper flat

edge, thus leaving a more even ring of adhesive than could be otherwise obtained. The soap is easily wiped off turntable afterwards.

The next day, or later, a thin ring of cement can be put on the glass slide and the ring adjusted in place. When hardened in a few days there will be perfect contact of cement and glass, with perfect contact of cement and ring, with a layer of elastic cement in between which is capable of absorbing any small variation under the exercise of pressure. A ring fixed in this way is likely to remain permanent if the further mounting operations are properly performed.

To pass on to sealing up the mount after filling, taking it in wrong order for the present. When the object is in the fluid and the cell full, the cover glass is rested, as for balsam mounting, on the edge and held with the fingers in the same way, but as the fluid is aqueous, it can take to the cleaned glass more readily if the cover glass be damp. This is best effected by breathing on the surface of the glass two or three times just before it is to be fitted in place. The fluid readily runs up the damp glass if the latter be lowered gently into place, the fluid should be present in the cell in just sufficient quantity to shew a convex surface, so that there is just a little too much. After dropping it on the top, the cover can be gently pressed down with a needle on to the rim of the cell and the excess fluid forced out. This can be absorbed with a small piece of blotting paper, presenting torn edges of the paper to the edges of the cell and tearing away the wet portions as one proceeds so as to get continually a dry edge to take up the excess fluid. The edges of the cell and the top of the cover can thus be dried. It can then be touched all around the junction of glass and rim with a little of the cement just described. In a quarter of an hour it can be put on the turntable and a clean even ring of the same cement floated on. The

cover glass must run truly to do this and the slide
must be adjusted under the clips till it runs centrally
before the cement is applied.   Another coat can be put
on the next day and a rim of black varnish a day or
two later and the slide labelled and stored.

Should there be any difficulty in fixing the cover on
to glass, it can be remedied in the way I recommend
for sealing a glycerine cell, as the cover glass holds
firmly enough to be ringed right away.

Procure a bottle of the well known " Diamond "
cement, which is a jelly when cold and needs standing
in hot water to soften for use.   When first bought
soften it in a cup of hot water and add four or five
drops of glycerine to prevent it ever hardening brittle
It will be ready for use then at any time.   Before filling the cell, but after cleaning it well out, put the
slide centrally on the turntable, and having the dia
mond cement warm, give the top of the rim, as it
revolves, a coating of the cement, making sure it
touches all over, but not too thick.   On the cold slide
it will set almost at once, leaving a thin elastic coating
on the top of the rim   This, in five minutes or so, will
be an elastic cushion on which the cover glass can
bed and be held with sufficient firmness to wipe dry
after pressing the glass into place   The cell can be
filled with fluid, and the object put in place without
the ring of diamond cement being at all in the way.   It
is partly gelatine, it is not soluble in the fluid used,
yet always remains tacky enough to hold the glass,
whilst offering no hindrance to the application of a
perfectly waterproof cement to effect a permanent seal,
which keeps the fluid in and the air out.   It is as well,
after cleaning the inside of a cell, and before proceeding
to fill it, to run it on the turntable and with a very
small sable brush paint the inside edge of the rim as
it revolves with a little of the mounting fluid   This
ensures the fluid filling the cell entirely and not leav-

ing, as would otherwise happen, a tiny space at the bottom edges unfilled, which would afterwards develop into a bubble in the preparation.

Of course, it is not possible to mount every whole insect in fluid on the ordinary size slide with a $\frac{3}{4}$ cover glass, but small insects mount whole this way. Any object mounted whole in a perceptible thickness of medium makes a better object for dark ground illumination with low powers, than objects which have been squeezed dead flat, because there is more room for the rays of light to be reflected downwards from the top side of the glass, and by that means illuminate the object. Hence, objects mounted in fluid make, as a rule, the best dark ground slides, as well as being more natural in appearance. It is well to prepare insects by putting them for a very short time in a weak caustic potash solution and afterwards in plain water, so that dirt, grease, or foreign substances can be cleaned off by gently brushing them with a soft camel hair brush. Being soft they can be arranged as nearly as possible in the desired attitude and then soaked in formalin solution for a few days. Then, when a sufficiently deep cell has been cleaned, prepared and filled with fluid just over the edge, the object to be mounted can be dropped in the fluid by the aid of a fine pair of tweezers, and arranged in position with a pair of needles. When adjusted in place, look at it with a hand magnifying glass to see that there is no dirt, hairs, fluff, or air bubbles present. If there be such, it must be removed before putting on the glass. If all is right, lower the cover glass slowly into place, and dry and edge it as previously directed.

Objects of an aquatic character being soft will not require the potash solution at all. They will just have to be brushed in plain water perfectly clean, and transferred at once to the formalin solution for soaking.

When the animal has retractile organs, which it is

desired to display as in life, it is necessary to narcotise
it before killing. Such things as the various rotifers
and the plumed polyzoa need this treatment, as otherwise they would look like a shapeless jelly rather than
" as in life." It is a delicate process, but if some of
these very tiny specks of animal life are found when
examined in the water trough, they can be made more
sluggish in their action by adding slowly at intervals,
one drop at a time, of a one per cent. solution of
cocaine or novocaine. This must be done carefully and
when they are almost quiescent Yet with their motile
organs extended, they can usually be killed with a drop
of saturated solution of corrosive sublimate, which kills
them instantly, before they can withdraw or shrivel up
This is rather advanced work, but beautiful slides can
be made by the method. For the usual case of small
flies, or parts of insects, such as head or legs, or any
part readily removed, not requiring delicate dissection,
the method of washing, soaking, and mounting is really
easier and shorter than balsam, once the art of sealing
the cell is acquired It has also the further advantage
that the cell can be opened and re-mounted, or object
re-arranged without great trouble.

Stem sections, any parts of plants; petals, fibres of
plants, leaves of water plants; filamentous alga, growing in gutters, mosses; nettle stings; hairs from
plants; aphides, which are the green and black fly so
beloved by the gardener, any water insect or larvæ;
tadpoles; and small spiders, etc., can all be mounted
by this process, which is recommended as being the
easiest, most satisfactory, and least trouble

Glycerine mounting is done in the same way as
above, but it wants more care and skill The objects
must be cleaned and left to soak in glycerine of the
same density as that to be used for the final mounting
As a general rule, objects contain water, and glycerine
has such an affinity for water, that if an object con-

taining much water and whose body is not very strong
be put directly into glycerine, the water is abstracted
with such violence that the object is distorted or broken
to pieces. Hence, it is necessary to proceed by easy
stages. The object is put into glycerine and water,
half each, for a few days. It is then transferred at
intervals to solutions containing more glycerine and
less water successively till by a gradual process pure
glycerine is reached. The mounting itself is not more
difficult, but the fluid being so heavy, it is much more
difficult to dislodge air-bubbles, as they do not, except
in very hot weather, rise to the surface, and even then
rise slowly. The sealing is accomplished most readily
by giving the cell a rim of diamond cement, as mentioned, and thoroughly washing away with a brush any
glycerine that has exuded from the cell. This should
be done under water, and if a clip be necessary to hold
the cover glass on, whilst washing it clean of glycerine,
the clip must be removed before the slide is taken above
the surface of the water. If a little water gets in,
owing to the pressure of clip being removed, it would
not matter, as it only slightly dilutes the glycerine.
If, however, the clip is removed above the water surface, air would enter instead of water, and the slide
would be spoiled. After removing from the water the
slide can be left to dry by itself, or can be dried with
blotting paper. As soon as the edge of cover is dry,
the sealing cement can be applied. Glycerine is a good
preservative, and is used either pure, or mixed with
water in various proportions. A mixture of half glycerine and half of the formalin solution is favoured by
some mounters.

Glycerine jelly is purchasable at the optician shops.
It is a pure gelatine, softened with water and glycerine
added. It hardens like glue or size to a jelly, and has
to be warmed for use. It is handled more like using
balsam, and the objects should previously be soaked in

H

pure glycerine, or glycerine and water. With a fountain pen filler a portion of the melted jelly is dropped
on a warmed slide, the object put in place and
arranged, a drop more melted jelly put on top, and
the cover glass applied.   When cold, the superfluous
jelly can be cut off with a small knife, the edges washed
clean from glycerine and the sealing cement ring put
on   All as before   A convenient way of using glycerine jelly is to work on a piece of tin, or a tin dish
over another dish filled with warm water   Unless the
object is thick a cell is not essential, as the jelly will
support the object and it can't run out. Permanent
mounts in this medium, however, are rare, and it does
not seem very popular

There are various fancies by different mounters as
to the preservative, and each believes his own formula
to be the best.   Possibly, that is because the favourite
material is most practised, and that is why one formula
had better be adhered to until sufficient dexterity is
acquired to warrant further experiment

Many delicate objects are well suited by camphor
water, others by weak carbolic acid solution, and others
by various preservative fluids   Some of these are
mentioned amongst recipes upon another page, but as
the opticians sell them already prepared, it is hardly
worth while compounding them oneself, unless for ex-
perimental purposes, as the quantities required by the
microscopist are so small   The materials to mix them
would probably cost as much as the prepared solutions,
which are sold filtered ready for use

When a mount containing fluid can be finished and
sealed, with a certainty that it neither leaks nor contains air, it is well to try various media as mountants
Many objects are really well displayed in one fluid
which do not look well in others, and some particular
feature or structure is more evident and more easily
seen,

Slides intended to be used with immersion lenses should always be given a final ringing of shellac in alcohol, as the immersion oil attacks all other ringing varnishes.

The following tools used in mounting will be needed Needles mounted in penholders, small scalpels and fine scissors if dissection is attempted, sable and camel hair brushes of various sizes; tweezers to pick up small objects; fountain pen fillers, glass with rubber bulb at end, for conveying balsam or fluid, and a turntable Messrs. Baker, of Holborn, sell a delicate pocket tweezer, devised by the writer, which should be very useful, as, being flexible, they will not damage a very delicate or fragile object, whilst it can be firmly held. Being in a pocket case like a pencil it will be found a useful companion either in the garden or on an outdoor ramble

For balsam mounting, a few spring clips to hold cover glass against any warping of the object, facilitate a well finished slide.

The above, with a small supply of 3 x 1 glass slips, some cover glasses, and a few labels, will complete the necessary outfit. The cost is not great, but the pleasure of mounting one's own objects give a zeal to life, and it can truly be said that after the hobby of microscopy be once started it is the cheapest and deepest form of recreation The running expenses and the deterioration of apparatus are quite infinitesimal The mental gain and the greater perception of the wonders of life are as great as the things regarded are small

CHAPTER XIV.

MOUNTING MATERIALS.

Cell cement —*Gold size.*—This should be thick and old.

Gold size, indiarubber and shellac —See page 108.

Ward's cement, as sold by opticians and dealers

Shellac in naphtha.—Brittle, but good for cells containing oil.

Ringing varnish to finish —*Gold size,* with enough good quality printer's ink to give right consistency. Should not be used too fluid.

Sealing wax, of desired colour, dissolved in methylated spirit   Liable to chip but brilliantly glossy

Finishing varnishes, as sold by dealers in all colours.

Preservation fluids.—*Formalin* 40 per cent , one part; distilled water 15 parts

Alcohol in water in equal proportions   Not methylated.

Crystallised carbolic acid in water —Acid one part, water 100 parts

Camphor water.—Tincture of camphor ¼ ounce Distilled water one quart   When mixed this becomes turbid   Allow to settle and pour off the perfectly clear solution only for use in mounting.   The cloudy can be used to preserve specimens which it is desired to mount at a future time

Pure glycerine —Good, but few objects can be put directly into it from water, as previously remarked. Objects, if not very delicate, can be put into equal parts of pure glycerine and alcohol, leaving the alcohol to evaporate by effects of time, when the preparation will be found permeated without distortion in the heavy glycerine

Glycerine can be used mixed in all proportions with formalin solution above, or camphor water as a mounting fluid When diluted is a little less trouble to manipulate.

If distilled water is unobtainable, use as a substitute, filtered rain water which has been boiled after filtering Tap water contains lime and other impurities which may set up cloudiness or air bubbles by chemical reactions

Goadby's fluid —Bay salt 2 oz , alum 1 oz., bichloride mercury 2 grains, and distilled water 1 quart. Filter after solution and keep for use.

For green algæ and pond weed.—Acetate of copper ¼ oz., camphor water half a pint.

Farrant's medium.—Clean gum arabic 2 oz., glycerine 1 oz , distilled water 2 oz A thick viscid medium.

Glycerine jelly —Nelson's gelatine 1 oz , glycerine ¾ oz , tincture of camphor ¼ oz Soak gelatine in water till it absorbs no more Drain away water not absorbed and melt the gelatine by standing bottle or jar containing it in another filled with hot water. When melted, add the glycerine and camphor Filter through fine flannel whilst hot Cools to a jelly and has to be warmed for use

All above can be purchased ready prepared under the names given, from dealers in mounting materials

Balsam in benzole, balsam in xylol, and all other requisites of the kind are sold in bottles

Bleaching fluid for objects too dense to mount on transparencies. Chloride of lime ¼ oz , water 1 pint. Mix and allow to settle, but only use the clear solution

Bleaching fluid No. 2.—Chlorate of potash 1 oz., water 1 pint Keep as a stock solution and add hydrochloric acid to the bath in which the object is immersed Leave it until it be sufficiently decolorised Two or three drops of acid to one ounce of stock solution.

Potash solution for softening and cleaning Caustic potash in sticks 1 oz , water 1 quart.

CHAPTER XV.

STORING SLIDES

After a few slides have been made, the time will arrive when some systematic method of storing them will be needed. Boxes and cases of various forms are to be had for this purpose   Some expensive, elaborate and ornamental, and some plain and cheap

There are boxes sold, which, holding 72 in 12 trays, will be found the more convenient. Additional boxes may be bought as desired, and when a number of slides are in the collection, they can be divided into classes and varieties and the box labelled on the outside.   The slides lie flat in trays, and the series in one tray can all be seen and the labels read at one time   Any specimen can be withdrawn or replaced without disturbing the others, and slides are not damaged by sliding over each other with the danger of spoiling the mounts.

By using these storage boxes the collection is always tidy, always at hand, always complete in appearance, yet capable of expansion by adding another box as the number of slides increases.

Avoid any store boxes which keep the slides edgeways, as any objects in fluid mounts will be likely to be put out of centre, and even in opaque mounts the small gummed object may be dislodged and the slide ruined

A slide should be gently and carefully cleaned from dust and dirt before using and wiped clean before putting it away.   Dirt magnified in the same field is unavoidable if it be inside the mount, but can easily be removed from the outside   A clean, bright image can only be secured from a clean, bright slide, and there need be no imperfect images because of outside dirt

INDEX.

CPSIA information can be obtained at www.ICGtesting.com
Printed in the USA
LVOW09s0214110913

351837LV00013B/310/P

9 781171 648581